A COVENANT FOR ALL SEASONS

A
COVENANT
FOR ALL
SEASONS

THE
MARRIAGE
JOURNEY

CALVIN MILLER

Harold Shaw Publishers
Wheaton, Illinois

ISBN 0-87788-386-6

Cover and inside design by David LaPlaca

Library of Congress Cataloging-in-Publication Data
Miller, Calvin.
    [If this be love]
    A covenant for all seasons : the marriage journey / Calvin Miller.
      p.   cm.
    Originally published: San Francisco : Harper & Row, c1984.
    ISBN 0-87788-386-6
    1. Marriage—Religious aspects—Christianity. 2. Christian life—
Baptist authors. 3. Miller, Calvin. 4. Miller, Barbara.
5. Baptists—Clergy—United States—Biography. I. Title.
BV835.M55 1995
248.4—dc20   95-7593
                                              CIP

02 01 00 99 98 97 96 95

Contents

If THIS BE LOVE

If this be love, expect me not to wait

One day to tell of it. For life is chance

And so unsure that I must celebrate

It while I have the strength to dance.

Here is integrity: If there be truth,

As I can know the time, the time is right.

The passing years have fed upon my youth.

The day to testify grows short of light.

I know the risk: Love could still prove a lie.

Some fickle future circumstance might kill

My best resolve: I do's so sometimes die.

Broken vows are spawned by weakened will.

Old promises must pledge themselves each day

Or, unrenewed, pass quietly away.

To Barbara

Love is delicate crystal. Yet, fragile as it is, every marriage begins with braggart promises in breathy ceremonies. Having never seen the future, love struts in candlelight and whispers in confidence: "Till death do us part." Yet the best love, I think, always makes its pledges without stopping to regard the strength of its ardor. Like all the rest, we once made such promises, surer at the threshold of marriage than we could ever be within that unexplored togetherness we have walked from anniversary to anniversary.

Now we know. Love is not a happening, but a discipline. It only grows by feeding on constant attention and effort. There have been times in the decades past that I wondered—even doubted—that I loved you. But doubt is not a sin in loving. Arrogance is the grand transgression, for arrogance presumes, and presumption loses all.

Love is a pilgrimage, and pilgrimages have many destinations. Therefore, a book like this risks everything! Either of us could, in time, abandon all our vows and shrug away those promises we once made. In such an hour we would disclaim everything we now endorse in joy.

Now, indeed, we honor all the promises we've made. And since we well know the penalty of neglect, we intend to discipline our lives and work at keeping those old promises. It is the old promises that are the easiest forgotten. The recent promises are nearer and more clamorous. Yet when the fire is low and we are much alone, I still hear those thirty-five-year-old words, and every time I hear them, recommit myself. My silent grin at these fireside reveries means that inwardly I am reinforcing those old vows with newer pledges. For in a world where nothing is safe, we owe each other the kind of risk we take. Here in the hurried days of mid-marriage, we are resolved. We are now, more than ever, committed to the discipline of loving. Ours is the declaration of pilgrims who have not finished the pilgrimage—though we are hopeful that its end will keep its present glory.

The Seasons of Love

Most of what I've learned and know for sure, I learned only yesterday. What I knew before yesterday was sporadic and untried. All of us suffer here and there in life from the dangerous presumption of thinking we know who we are. We foolishly suppose we have lived with ourselves long enough to know our own definition. But self-introspection alone can never provide that definition. Throughout our lives others are the mirror to ourselves—the only mirror. All we ever see of ourselves, before we stumble on this critical mirror, is an uncertain egoistic reflection—a fun-house image in warped glass and twisted quicksilver.

So I have come to know myself only by looking into that mirror you hold up to me. Only there, reflected in your love, can I really see myself. Because I have no other way of figuring out exactly who I am, I know why God said to Adam, "It is not good for a man to be alone" (Gen. 2:18).

I have asked myself many times during these thirty-five years: Are "we" the same "us" that stood and made promises to love and honor and cherish in 1959? Yes, in some ways. But in other ways, time and grief and joy have shaped us into two souls who only faintly resemble those long-ago, teen-age promise-makers.

But the circumstances of our union have been the painful benefactors of our gradual transformation. As Augustine said, God's grace sometimes visits us with a severe mercy. Our once willowy convictions have been toughened into an iron-wood mace for ruling life. We both know how it happened. The toughness was fashioned by the pain. It is the breaking of each woody fiber that makes the willow into steel at last. With every mountain storm that whips the pliant juniper against the muddy earth, the fibers break, and the inner scars of its twisted trunk learn a manganese resilience that only brokenness can teach.

When most of these lessons came to our lives, we protested the pain. We railed against the very storms that made us strong. That's how it is with marriages. They are either made strong by testing or weak through smoother circumstances. Easy living can curse a marriage with competition. Those couples who never bend their souls to face a common foe often name each other as the enemy.

God is a great friend of marriage. He rarely blesses couples with complete tranquillity. Rather, He is all-gracious and sends severer mercies. He sends the fire that burns us into dependent loneliness and utter need. His fire burns, but it is always better than the bland and painless prosperity that produces only a creeping callousness. Struggle is the gracious stuff that saves two people from that numb functioning they might otherwise call marriage.

In these pages I want to rehearse again the events of our lives that have made our marriage strong. They were never the events we prayed for. We asked God for what we wanted and were always given what we needed. We asked God to spare us pain so we could enjoy our lives, but he so often gave us pain that we might become real. What were these maturing events?

They were different for each of us. For you, the greatest pain often came in terms of our family needs. I suspect I suffered most often because I could never reconcile my expectations of church members with their actual behavior. I knew I lived out my own faith somewhat imperfectly, but I often ran against some awful congregational hypocrisy that lay unseen beneath the sacred surface of phony decorum. I always envied those intuitive powers by which you spotted hypocrisy before it disclosed itself. Christian villainy rarely surprised you, and seeing it ahead of time always enabled you to pass by those potholes of disappointment into which I fell headlong. You warned me then set me free for these inevitable falls. Yet you never said, "See there," or "I told you." I happily chirp my way to guillotines. I have never been able to see the Dr. Hyde in all the Henry Jekylls that promised me their love and support.

Your pain, on the other hand, came when the funds were too short to buy the children the minimal clothes they needed to endure the coming Nebraska winters (thank goodness you sewed). You hurt when the pantry was too bare to endure the month left over at the end of the money (thank goodness you cooked). You hurt when I had to appear at some august occasion in a cheap suit (thank goodness you were a wizard at retailoring).

But we made it. We are the survivors who watched God fashion our stumbling blocks into stairways. And while we've reached no great plateaus of human celebration, we are well at the moment. We also know love: Our children love us, and our grandson has given us a glorious reason to push into the future with bright prospects.

To say we are happy is to say too little; we are more than that. To say we are secure is too presumptuous, for who knows what tomorrow may require? But to say we're together and confident in Christ is just right. We know that God will supply all our needs and that whatever our circumstances, we can be content (Phil. 4:12, 19). And though the floods of life may come and the waters of life threaten us, our favorite Scripture still stands: "Many waters cannot quench love, neither can the floods drown it: if a man would give all the substance of his house for love, it would utterly be contemned" (Song of Sol. 8:7). Our favorite hymn bears witness that the terrors ahead of us can never be as great as the love behind us.

> *Great is thy faithfulness, O God, my Father.*
> *Morning by morning new mercies I see;*
> *All I have needed thy hand hath provided.*
> *Great is thy faithfulness, Lord, unto me!*

Everything considered, I love you now and always will. I'm quite content to let Shakespeare conclude it all for me, whatever may come:

> *For thy sweet love remember'd such wealth brings*
> *That then I scorn to change my state with kings.*

PERSPECTIVE

Three decades past I skipped along beside
Her. Soul tired—I carried grain and grumbled.
How tall she looked! How large the fields! Her stride
Was smooth. Attempting to keep pace, I stumbled.
She sat the grain where all the grass seemed dead,
And ran her fingers through my tangled thatch.
"Some day the fields will seem so small," she said.
"When you've grown large, the fields will be no match."
"The fields are very big," I said. "You'll see!"
She grinned and kissed my immaturity.
Our shadows were El Greco-esque as we
Trudged across the endless earthen sea.
She sleeps beneath those fields where she stood tall.
And I, at last, can see the fields are small.

CHAPTER ONE

The First First-Lady

She came before you, not in prominence but in time. Yet in every way she readied me to love you. To say this woman's image would be stamped upon your being may seem a monstrous strike against your uniqueness. Yet here I must begin. I knew her first: not just before I knew you, but before I knew anyone. First knowledge emerges unsteady in the haze of infancy. It is umbilical, inseparate. What is it I remember of her? Some husky alto lullaby? Perhaps. I remember and yet do not. Life is dim and distant when it emerges from the womb. It is separate from motherhood, yet too amniotic to be very separate . . . an embryonic reverie of gray amnesia . . . a thereness not yet there. Remembering is not the issue; it is life. Being was her gift.

Still, being has to wait to understand, to know itself. Being comes from the shadows and moves only gradually toward the light. Without a sense of being, my knowledge of myself was not "mine" but "ours." The two of us were there as far back as it is possible to probe the fringes of memory.

She was there some twenty years before you. She was there when my father left—when the bombs shattered the balmy air above faraway Hawaii. With her covey of little ones and no means of support except her two good hands, her strong intention was to serve. She vowed that her life would give life to her brood of nine.

I don't know that she was brave, but I remember her as fearless. I believe she saw fear as an unnecessary tremulous contagion. Fear was always contracted in dread and spread by those who volunteered to quake. If she was afraid, I never knew it. In her confident presence, I grew up braver than I might have been.

I never knew I was poor, either. From time to time, there are those who do spin straw into gold. She was one of those who could create a sense of strong abundance from the thinnest poverty.

The house my father left to us was unfinished. However, not knowing what a finished house looked like, I was not aware of its uncompleted state. I could tell it was small—three rooms and no indoor plumbing. We burned wood when the Oklahoma winter was short, and coal when it was not.

My mother was such a pragmatist that none of us ever viewed her as a miracle worker. Wood ranges were supposed to yield hot berry pies and overflow with yeasty loaves of bread. For countless winters I stood before that iron icon and learned that abundance is never what we have but what we suppose we have. I was rich because my mother seemed rich and I never saw the actual poverty of those days.

At Christmas, she would read Dickens's Christmas stories by the light of a kerosene lamp—which we called a "coal-oil" lamp. With never so much as a goose of our own for Christmas dinner, we all felt sorry for the Cratchits. In the midst of a life that others viewed as desperate and hard, my mother's inner wealth was a spirit so abundant that it fostered and made real a luxuriant deception: I too was rich.

Still, thrift is the kinsman to wealth. Nothing was to be thrown away. I only later saw the wonderful wealth she demonstrated. Life was an economy! Subtle were her greatest lessons. She gave dignity to thrift. She taught all her children to feel pride in constructing the indispensable from things others threw away. A rummage sale bristled with opportunities to keep the winter warm. Secondhand clothes were not vile items cast away by others. Hand-me-downs from my two older brothers were an opportunity to wear things that had already twice proven themselves worthy. There were wonderful things all about us that, in their simplicity, were usable, and left us no need to frequent pretentious shops. Those stores were for people with limited ingenuity.

She also taught us that we were only managers of heaven's gifts. The Lord provided everything. Our daily bread had come from Him, my mother said, and like manna, it lay on the ground to be taken fresh every morning.

Our house backed up to "the tracks." The great locomotives ran only an alley away from our rough-weathered dwelling. The tracks were the parallel footprints of the mammoth dragons that stalked the land in which I lived. The trains came day and night, and left me dreaming by the steel rails. I much romanticized the great locomotives. Enraptured, I waved at the engineers who rode the iron dragons like powerful warlords on armored beasts.

I think she knew how my reveries constructed dragons from these "puffer-bellies" that drew strings of namby-pamby cars along the silver strands. Some said the tracks went all the way to St. Louis and ended in Los Angeles, but neither of these suppositions intrigued me. The rails held a mysterious enchantment of their own. The tracks were real; so were the steel dragons. So real that their heavy iron wheels would flatten pennies to the size of silver dollars. Those same iron wheels sent earthquakes up and down the line as the grumbling steam rattled every window in our tiny house.

But the tracks were not dreaming places to her. While I celebrated their intrigue, she celebrated their gravel beds in which the cross ties, splintered by the spikes, held more than rails. The old wooden cars jolted and banged around during harvest. They would leak, and their spillage was the manna—the daily bread—the windfall to our economy.

She would take a pail and a broom and go to the tracks to sweep the spilled grain, and I would accompany her. The grain we found not only fed our meager flock of chickens, but was a staple in our diet as well.

When the cars were full of wheat, so indeed were the rusty barrels behind our house where we stored the grain we had retrieved from the leaky cars. At harvest time, we worked at gathering the immense piles of trackside grain. I despised the practicality rooted in her thrift. Yet her mundane view of the tracks held life for all her little ones.

I know now it is sometimes necessary to make trains out of dragons and demythologize strings of cars until we can see a kind of life in them. I took the bread for granted and supposed that it only existed to nourish

my imagination. Out of my mother's practical con-
cerns came the bread for dreaming, and she knew that
dreams would all degenerate to poverty if her little
ones went hungry.

I was the seventh child, born just after the older
children had absorbed the slow-departing pain of the
Great Depression. Her firstborn was barely eight when
Black Tuesday occurred. In her painful management of
life during the "dirty" thirties, she tirelessly celebrated
the warm abundance of even that improvident provi-
dence. She knew life could be handled; harvest would
come. There would be wheat between the rails.

"We are the gleaners," she seemed to say as we
crossed the fields on the way home from the "far
tracks." This was a second spur a mile or so from our
home, and we gleaned the distant rails as well as those
at hand. The distant rails were always the most fruit-
ful: since the old cars sat there longer, their spillage
was more abundant. Thus we crossed the wider fields
carrying sacks or pails to gather all the grain we could.

I hated the work. There was little romance in lifting
the chubby burlap sacks of grain. The drudgery of
such toil crushed my imagination into powder. Reluctantly I was learning to trade enchantment for bread.

They say every son marries his mother, and though I
cannot prove this proverb, it does seem to me now that
you and my mother were remarkably alike. You both

loved things that should be, but not too much to deal with things that must be. It has always been my nature to dream the turbulence from whirlpools. You, like her, could see so well the troubled waters I denied. How much I've had to trust the both of you to tell me where my visions could not swim through cold reality. Yet your honesty, like hers, was compassionate. Her greatness once protected a child, and your greatness, the visions of a too-reluctant man.

And yet, the fond distinction between the child and the man I learned by walking the fields and crossing "the tracks." I cannot, as the apostle Paul suggests, put away these childish things because I have become a man. A thousand times no! For in such childish things is wisdom rooted. I know that in the crossing of those distant fields, my manhood was defined.

CHILD OF ARMAGEDDON

A child of holocaust will cry for space

To hide. Despair and insecurity

Make children run and whimper to embrace

Some thread of hope and worthy sovereignty—

I read of war and distant enemies:

I, Armageddon's child, whose joyless rhyme

Was sung in nuclear Gethsemanes,

Where doomsday was the looming foe of time.

Christ came to be a midwife in the fray

As I dropped womb-ward towards the Trinity.

My childhood knew the birth of God. The day

He came, the vacuum died. Infinity

Was reckless joy and braggart bright

As I, with titan stride, stepped out of night.

CHAPTER TWO

The Coming of Light

My childhood was set in troubled times. There were wars and rumors of wars.

I remember newspapers as the stark tabloids of conflict. My imagination ached from the images of death that every one of them contained. By 1943, all four of my older sisters were newly married to U.S. servicemen. The security of their husbands was an unceasing concern in our family. We spoke of little else at mealtime. I learned the weight of the word *war* as our family dealt with it from day to day.

Mostly it was the newsprint pictures that troubled me. When I looked at those photographs, I could no longer change steam engines into dragons. The tracks had become barren, and all of us seemed no longer bright pilgrims but disillusioned refugees from better times.

The papers came and went. I regularly asked my mother about the newsprint pictures. Why war? Why armies? Why bombs? Why do the Japanese hate the Americans and the Americans hate the Germans? Why do the Germans want to kill Jews? Why all these pictures of death? Why death?

I remember that in my sickness of heart, I clung to my mother and waited to know what justification there could be. Then came the bold headlines and the big pictures: D-day, V-E Day, and finally V-J Day.

Two events marked my life in the year 1945. Both came in the month of August.

Four-syllable Japanese cities were eradicated by a three-syllable U.S. bomb. Terror and radiation were words I learned quickly, if reluctantly.

"The war is over at least—at last. Your sisters' husbands will all be home—and not a one of them was lost!"

"But the pictures!"

"They will pass," she said. "The pictures will change."

Thinking of the August papers, I asked, "Momma, did the bomb float on a parachute?"

"They say it did."

I watched the maple seeds that summer twist in the dry wind and sail and spin like the propellers of P38s and Flying Tigers. I knew the names of planes for they, too, were in the papers, and I watched the seeds fall and thought of the great canopy of the chute that settled over the children of Japan until finally the blossom erupted into fire that seared the city and its children into silence. I hated the papers and at last would look at them no longer.

Still, I dreamed on and on about the settling of the bomb.

In later years, when you and I had become committed each to the other, I would know the Bible. I would learn in seminary that God was sovereign over men and nature. But 1945 was a year charged with the spirit of Apocalypse. I went to a small church where I learned the popular adventist truth that Jesus Christ was coming again. The events that preceded His coming would terrify and astound even the Pentecostals who attended the small, weathered meetinghouse. The fiery sermons of visiting evangelists held images that, to my own young mind, seemed too much like the fire storms of Dresden or Nagasaki.

One night, I walked down to the armory to watch a softball game. A childhood chum who accompanied me had also listened to the doomsday sermons of the

Pentecostal evangelists. He delighted in their fiery sermons and listened much closer than I did. He told me all about the horrible anti-Christ who, he said, would begin World War III.

"We will all be forced to wear the mark of the beast," he assured me. "Right on our foreheads, too!" I was terrified by the idea of the beast and his mark. At nine years of age, my friend seemed over delighted by his prophecies. "Oh yes," he almost salivated like a young Jeremiah, and he wagged his little finger. "Those bombs that fell on Nagasaki are only the beginning! Bombs are going to fall everywhere!" He left off preaching doom as he leaned against the wire mesh of the backstop at the softball field. I began to feel sick as he pressed on in his determination to enlighten me about the end of the world.

He asked me if I had ever heard of the book of Revelation. When I told him that I had not, he informed me that the book of Revelation told of the Battle of Armageddon: "Human blood will run up to the horses' bridles," he said. The horror of his prophecy, coupled with the pictures I had seen so lately in the papers, was too much for me. It was more than my child's psyche could bear.

I burst into tears and cried all the way home from the ballpark. Nothing of beauty remained to me. I was a man in the making, but manhood did not seem a worthy goal. When men were grown, they dropped bombs on other men and photographed the devastation, letting everyone behold the horror.

"Momma," I said when I arrived home, "will there be blood up to the horses' bridles?"

"When? What do you mean?" she asked.

I could not go on with the questions, and I was sure I could not face her answers. Yet the image was there and has not left me for the greater part of four decades.

In time, you and I would meet as survivors of these visions. Together we would live through the nuclear omen of the Cuban Missile Crisis. Later, we would fill our own bathtub with water and stock our pantry with meager supplies, supposing the days of our young marriage would give way to universal bloodshed. In our early marriage, we would thus commit ourselves each to the other, daring the evil to come. We, like those around us, gradually grew easier with images of nuclear destruction. We had to live with those images. We could have no happiness unless we let our laughter push the Apocalypse away.

The Armageddon symbol that came to me at a softball game in 1945 left me sweltering under a dismal proposition. Horses' bridles were pretty high up to a nine year old. Mine was a youthful, naive battle with

Pentecostal existentialism. Still, I think I knew from that night, I hungered for some alternate path of life.

My chum who had gone with me to the game could not understand my madness. There have always been people like him who can be casual about terror. On the other hand, he felt I was over serious about the issue of war. I could not understand his passivity; the horror he described for me at the softball game did not even interrupt the snowcone he was eating at the time. His chilling exuberance had its effect. I knew I didn't want to grow up to be a person who enjoyed gore. I never wanted to become one of those savages whose greatest dreams for the world whistled through holocausts, occupying themselves with business as usual. What would Armageddon really be like? When would it come? Would the fiery exhibition catch us at softball leagues and snowcones? Later I would read what T. H. White summed up through Merlin's lips: "Man is not *Homo sapiens*, 'man the knowing,' but *Homo ferox*, 'man the savage.' "

I knew what I wanted: not just to survive, but a reason to survive. There were too many thorns in the nest, and my discomfort led me to many questions.

There must be another race, another kind of people. Indeed, there must be another kind of world whose newspapers arrive each morning to celebrate human dignity. Wherever that world was, it would be presided over by a kind God who did not believe in war nor permit it for others.

Where was that world?

Where was that race?

My imperfect perceptions were soon to dissolve in an important discovery as beautiful as the prophecy was ugly. As this new world view became mine, I found the only sanity that exists. With this discovery, reason and meaning both rose in elemental ways to become mine.

Can one feel all of these things at nine years? Does not maturity read back into the past things that the interim years lead us to forget? Of course, to some degree this must be true, and now, as a man, I cannot remember how I felt so long ago—at least all that I felt. But the rudiments of these years are real to me—the pain of seeing the papers and reckoning with war. The intensity of my juvenile despair was also real—accentuated by the times I saw my mother fold one of her hands in the red-white knuckles of the other, asking God to bring her children's husbands home.

Later in August of 1945 came a second life-changing event. I went to a tent revival set up in an open field near my home. Dressed in denim overalls that all children customarily wore, I sat on a plank supported by concrete blocks. I shuffled my naked feet through the new wood shavings that served as a floor for the tabernacle. The aroma of the newly sawn wood fibers that filtered through the tattered canvas of the revival tent brought an exhilaration of spirit.

It was years before I would behold the Gothic cathedrals of Europe. In my provincial view, the great tent was a great church. The hymns were as happy as the brotherhood was exhibitionist. Here I found a reprieve from a world too much burdened by the heaviness of Nagasaki and ballpark prophecy. The sawdust seemed sweet and safe and warm to my bare feet. It was a haven where they sang of heaven.

"When we all get to heaven," they sang. Was this the other world I sought? Was it bomb-proof?

Perhaps the hymn was escapist. Perhaps it prevented those who sang from dealing seriously with their troubled world. But its logic offered a kind of healing to my mind. Here was a world for me. Could pearly gates and golden streets be any sweeter than sawdust aisles and amber canvas? The electric lights shined out through the tent making it look like a happy canvas jack-o-lantern. They sang of a "haven of rest" and I knew it was true. I had found a Pentecostal stopover that was an oasis in my parched Armageddon. What a gallant, warless world! This other land was a safe place, a place for dreaming and living and being men. In joy I heard them sing of it.

When we all get to heaven,
What a day of rejoicing that will be!
When we all see Jesus,
We'll sing and shout the victory!

I have a friend who refers to such music as being "blood-of-the-Lamby." Now, I know that it was not the great music of the church. Then, however, it held an answer I needed. Soon they sang an altar call. Even that was utopian music to my ears.

Two great ladies in "flour-sack" dresses, rotund as they were earnest, showed me "the way to Jesus." It was a way I was all-too-eager to walk. There, in the smell of new sawdust, I met the Christ who shortly became the pier of my new faith.

Inner light arrived.

They told me Christ had "saved my soul," but I knew it was far better than that. It was not my soul only He had saved, but my whole world view. Despair fled. The newspapers could no longer extinguish hope. Holocaust had an answer: He was there, and He was mine.

Two Lovers—One Will

She gave me life and He extended it.

She saved me from the cold and He from sin.

She taught me hope and He defended it.

From her I once was born . . . from Him, again.

She let me skip in fields that He had made.

He bid me bless the loaves she baked for me.

She ordered me to gaze where He once lay.

He bid me kneel in her Gethsemane.

I owe them both the treasures of my art

And am myself so saddled with my debt

I cannot fail in paying every part

Lest I should leave this pair with one regret.

A humble woman made me love a King.

In both of them was hidden everything.

CHAPTER THREE

Cruel Affections

My sixteenth year came, and still I was ignorant of your existence. You were eleven years old and growing up in another rural Oklahoma town some twenty-five miles distant—so close and yet a hemisphere away! The red shale roads of Oklahoma were soon to give way to asphalt. Until then our worlds would be unconnected, our lives separate.

My need to know you was circumvented not only by unpaved roads, but by my mother and Christ. Each of them had demanding things for me to do. Each of them held impossible dreams for me.

The demands of my sixteenth year became grievous. She began to talk to me about a career, which I sometimes saw as a ploy to force me out of the home. I

19

resented her continual nudging me to the edge of the nest. When I peered over the rim of her demands, I was frightened. I had always preferred life within the locked gates of my own privacy where I was sure of the terrain. Within this warm cloister, I had escaped from the cold sociology of grammar school and the wilderness of high school. Physically, I was all angles and thin lines. In contrast to my own underdeveloped self-image, it seemed that the athletes in our small city had community esteem and wide acceptance. They were stars not only at sports, but all of life; they ran past my thin shadow in every high-school corridor of adolescence. I was never good at athletics. Perhaps this was because I never had known a father to cheer such interests. Further, I resented my high school years in a system where only athletes held esteem. Mandatory physical education was a four-year course in violence for me. I was good at the language arts, but Latin scholarship gained no respect in our small Oklahoma school. Thus, my self-esteem developed improperly.

I clung tightly to my insecurities in an attempt to avoid choosing a risky career. In truth, I had no idea what I could do or what I might be good at. Most of the boys I knew smoked Lucky Strikes and talked about joining the Marines. My own skeletal profile was not generally what one saw in the recruiting posters of "fighting leathernecks."

I could think of no suitable career, and my own desire to succeed outside the nest was less than my desire to stay warm within it.

Still, she pushed.

To escape from her, I fled to Him. The little church I attended was one in which everyone prayed in a kind of Elizabethan tongue, and so did I. "What wilt Thou?" I prayed. Adolescent Gethsemanes often seem trivial gardens to adults. I sought an answer that would deliver me from her harsh pushing. Seeing my tendency to hide from the future, He kept asking me what I intended to do with my life. He met me one night in the sixth chapter of Isaiah:

> In the year that king Uzziah died I saw also the Lord sitting upon a throne, high and lifted up, and his train filled the temple. Above it stood the seraphims: each one had six wings; with twain he covered his face, and with twain he covered his feet, and with twain he did fly. And one cried unto another, and said, Holy, holy, holy, is the Lord of hosts: the whole earth is full of his glory (6:1-3).

Isaiah too was an adolescent when he received his calling at the funeral of King Uzziah. He also felt a little pushed around by God. He, too, drew back from God's agenda.

It was not hard for me to admit my teen-age reluctance, but it was of some comfort to think of Isaiah as he ran full face into the holiness of God. He, too, must have felt weak before its high-altar demand.

This Scripture was twenty-eight hundred years old! I couldn't believe it! It was hard for me to accept that for twenty-eight centuries, God had been badgering timid adolescents with big demands. What right did He have to go around personally terrifying teenagers? I wondered.

And the posts of the door moved at the voice of him that cried, and the house was filled with smoke (6:4).

It must have been hard for Isaiah to go against such celestial fireworks and survive. It must have been frightening to talk to God while He was fuming and fussing in the fire. It was clear that God had something to say to me, but how could I know what He wanted? Even if I knew what He wanted, could I manage it? The will of God has never been as hard for me to obey as to locate. I found no rest. The Land of Oz loomed large. Unlike Dorothy, however, I found no yellow brick road.

"God, please, if You can't show me the road, at least give me the direction. I'm afraid I will disappoint both You and my mother," I bargained.

She was demanding that I leave the nest; He, that I be a minister. Neither of them let me live through my final year of high school in peace. I loved them both, but I could turn to neither of them for understanding. She wanted the difficult; He, the impossible.

I graduated from high school at last and hired on to a traveling harvest crew. I ignored her by leaving home and read widely around Isaiah 6 to ignore Him. I drove a huge grain truck from the sandy fields of northern Oklahoma across the wheat fields of Kansas, Nebraska, and South Dakota.

My thin frame never thickened, but I began to pick up a wiry mental toughness that summer. My mind was ill at ease. I knew that driving a truck would not be worthy of those gifts she believed I had. Further, Christ was not satisfied, and I knew it. He was that inescapable "Hound of Heaven." In the wheat fields of South Dakota, as I bent my naked back scooping the harvest, He spoke to me so straightforwardly that my own sweat mingled with the gall of His propositions. Shoveling grain was easy compared to what He asked. The wheat, ripe and abundant, poured like water from the spouts of our combines across four states. I found I could not leave either Him or His demands in Oklahoma. He met me in Kansas—and shouted out above the roar of my truck in Nebraska. In South Dakota, the wheat harvest only suggested that other harvest of which He spoke in the gospels. His fields were also white unto harvest. The harvest over which He was Lord, I had ignored.

August came.

Why did everything always happen to me in August? It was a full nine years after Nagasaki, but my madness was as furious as ever. The harvest was over and I left South Dakota, returning home. She who once taught me to carry grain across the wide fields was waiting.

She reminded me that it was only a couple of weeks till the opening of the university. I told her to back off, for I was still reckoning with Him. I told her I would have to make up my own mind. Gradually, however, I acquiesced.

I took a small suitcase and the three hundred dollars I had earned driving a wheat truck that summer. She and I walked to the bus station late in August.

I couldn't speak, and she didn't. He was silent as well. I was so afraid as to be nearly morose. I bought my ticket, kissed her good-bye, and climbed into the diesel bus. I waved at her from the window, and the bus lurched out into the thin Oklahoma traffic.

They had won!

With no real hope of meeting either of their expectations, I was headed toward the university. The wheels
ground their heavy rubber into the seeping August
asphalt as I rode into a future I doubted would ever
please either of them. A grasshopper splatted on the
windshield of the bus.

"It's absurd," I said aloud above the diesel churning
of the smoky bus. Isaiah 6:8 loomed large:

*Also I heard the voice of the Lord, saying, Whom shall I
send, and who will go for us? Then said I, Here am I;
send me.*

THE HYDRA

I trembled, waiting for the beast to come.

Afraid, afraid, afraid, I always kept

My eyelids closed. My sluggish tongue was dumb,

Silent as a soul controlled, inert I slept.

We seldom have the courage to confess

The sin of fear whose austere face is grave,

Who rips us from security's caress

And leaves us lonely in the grottoes. Brave

At last, my ego drew its blade! Light burst

Upon my life. At once—it flooded in

Whitewashing sooted gloom. I swung. The cursed

Demon head fell at my feet. My thin

Esteem was barbed with spikes—half-hid, immersed

In fear, till I, flesh-torn and bruised, did win.

CHAPTER FOUR

A Muted Monster

You were not quite thirteen and I was almost eighteen. Our life together was drawing near. My quixotic tilting at giants seemed real. But like Quixote, I never discovered what windmills were until all the jousting was over. I had one demon that needed to be exorcised—an ogre that had no voice, for its tongue had been ripped away by fear. I could not speak in public.

This denizen guarded the way to my profession, determined I should never enter. The terror of speaking in public let me view myself only in a comic glass. The fear of this mute phantom of public embarrassment taught me to despise myself. I became very aloof, always wanting friendship—but afraid of rejection.

I enrolled in Speech 101 precisely because I was afraid to speak. I rarely mustered the courage even to ask a question in the class. I set out on each new assignment in public speaking with a firm resolve to conquer those fears, but my resolutions always ended in failure. If the seraphim of Isaiah had purged my lips, they had not enabled them. My greatest defeats came in the fear of what I knew His calling was:

Go, and tell this people, Hear ye indeed, but understand not; and see ye indeed, but perceive not (Isa. 6:9).

"Telling" may have been a strength for Isaiah, but it was not an attribute of mine. *Preaching* was a demon word, and I decided that the ego force required in preaching might be less than required in teaching. Teaching as a career profession was, therefore, much more attractive to me. Either one, however, still required public speaking. For the first eighteen weeks of my university studies, I lived in terror of that speech class.

I had always been taught that self-consciousness was a form of egoism. I knew even then that I lived too much inside myself, but I was so tied by feelings of doubt and inferiority that I could not find any liberation from my own weak self-image. I was not able to cope. I always began with bravado and found myself stammering and giving way to failure and embarrassment. My halting inadequacies were a pain not only for myself but for the class as well.

Because of Christ and my mother, I felt compelled to face the ordeal, even though the agony of the dilemma plunged me into continual depression. My speeches were always manuscripted and they read fairly well. But my delivery of them was a stammering exercise in humiliation.

Mercifully, the end of the semester came and the course with it. My professor promised to pass me if I promised never to enroll in any of her advanced courses. Foolishly I promised, only to break the promise because of inner spiritual pressure. I shall long remember her crestfallen look when I walked back into her Speech 102, determined to do better than I had done in her Speech 101.

Again the humiliation. Again the awful pressure to resign the course and yet never to resign.

My madness distilled in neurosis. I prayed for courage—the prayer went unanswered. Fear, like cancer, is best cured in the early stages. My struggle was all the more intense because I had waited so long to deal with it. All through high school I had retreated and withdrawn from any position of visible responsibility.

I knew I had to learn public speaking. But whenever I considered that I might be facing this horror throughout life, despair settled all the more about me.

Several times during the second semester I tried to quit the course. At every plateau of despondency, Christ came, insisting that I keep on. I did not want His presence, for it reminded me of my unfulfilled desire to please Him. Like Francis Thompson, I sought to elude the elusive "Hound of Heaven":

> *I fled Him, down the nights and down the days;*
> * I fled Him, down the arches of the years;*
> *I fled Him, down the labyrinthine ways*
> * Of my own mind; and in the midst of tears*
> *I hid from Him, and under running laughter.*

I wish I could report some dramatic experience or breakthrough. I cannot.

If there was one single tactic that delivered me, it had to do with the image in my mirror. My professor, whose patience had grown threadbare and whose nerve endings were as raw as my own, told me never to come to class with a speech that I had not practiced out loud at least ten times before a mirror. Videotape was still hiding in the future, so the playback system I used was a looking glass. But there I discovered a third and powerful force that was a determinant of destiny—and I could not turn away from it.

There was in my mirror an angular face, molded like my mother's and energized with His purpose, yet different from both. The chin was not weak—not really—nor was the eye. There was a strong lip and sufficient volume of air that lifted hefty syllables without even breathing hard. I practiced the speech, and my face agreed in strength with the strong content.

That's what was wrong! I had seen my mother's face, so often disappointed as it floated ghostlike before my mind's eye. I had seen His face, lit by the unsteady flickering of my inconstant trust and fear of failure. But I had never seen my own face.

To look at one's own face is to see into the future. Yes, there was something there. Once I saw it I named it after my own unique strength of character. The vision came all at once.

At last I was able to speak my speech to the glass "trippingly on the tongue." I tried, as Hamlet advised his players, not to "saw the air" with gestures that did not suit the actions. Soon the weak face I only thought was mine eroded. In its place were blue-green eyes, enrapt with their own reflection. The hypnosis of a rising ego at long last looked past the weaknesses.

Before my mirror, four eyes gathered into two pairs and my reflected self stared hard and powerfully at my real self. In some ways, I was born before that glass. I came at last into self-hood, struggling to be free from every need of approval by others. Once free of the need of it, I received my self in fullness.

I have had so many sincere Christians tell me that the ego of a Christian should be annihilated, so only Christ can live in its place. What an unhealthy pietism that is! A theology for worms, not men. Ego is our primal being, and when it is crushed, human life despairs its nobility and makes us less than God does. Suddenly neither Christ nor my mother were present—only I was there. Alone. I stared strength into the weak image I had taken to the glass.

At once I realized the truth of what St. Bernard had said: We love no one until we love ourselves. Only when we love ourselves can we forget about ourselves enough to love anyone else. Then and then alone can we be free enough to love God or man. Christ was not angered that I had learned to act alone. It was His demand. My usefulness to Him would be determined by my ability to stand and, in His name, to face the beast, whether I felt His presence or not.

I stood at last to speak as one made new. My eyes searched for an object, no longer content with seeing faces. Now my eyes needed to see other eyes. Eyes are the light of faces. Eyes are the beacons of thought, the mirrors to the mind, the gauges of interest, the shuttered windows of the soul.

I saw, and I was free. My eyes first grabbed the professor's, and I threw a paragraph of content into those wide and unbelieving apertures. Her eyes grew even wider when my words did not dissolve in stammering. I released my hypnotic beginning with my professor's eyes only to grab others. They, too, opened their vision to sip the vision of my own. In fury, my own face stalked its image in the faces of all those who filled the classroom. I was real. I knew the truth at last! I didn't have to pass speech, but I had to *become*. Surely He knew. For He did not want me to anguish in that nothingness that would honor neither of us. Alone I had won.

I sat down. My ordeal was over! The hydra slain!

In this discovery of myself, I was free to love. Naturally, as only God knew then, I was free to meet you on the firm and sturdy threshold of myself.

Of Certainty and Doubt

You came to me, for I was less convinced

Than you that you and I were meant to be.

How could you know that confidence you sensed

Would justify your sense of prophecy?

I felt the impact of each quality

You owned . . . your ancestry . . . your vibrant love

Of laughter and your firm, unbending plea

That marriages like ours were made above.

What was the chemistry I must have missed?

How could I doubt what you found so secure?

I wanted your assurance when we kissed

That all our fiery pledges would endure.

My unbelieving love I knew must grow.

I kissed and doubted—starved to love and know.

CHAPTER FIVE

The New Year

B y my twentieth year, Korea's quarreling halves had grown stable at the thirty-eighth parallel, and the Russians were into space. These "little" issues were less important to me than my newfound confidence in myself. A year had passed since I had earned my first pleasing marks in speech and communication. The office at the Student Alliance of Ministry had even found some opportunities for me to preach. Most of my early preaching was done in rural pulpits where there was no full-time minister. I wanted these pulpit experiences. Indeed, I knew I needed them. With each preaching assignment, my insecurity lessened. Preaching was not easy for me, since I still continued to memorize each sermon before a mirror. My preparation style was more like that of an actor rather than a pastor. Hours of tedious preparation were involved in getting myself ready for every sermon. But it was on one of these pulpit assignments that my life leaped into the future.

I met you.

It was not love at first sight. I cannot say that I even considered love at all when first we met, but the embryo of our relationship was created.

The last summer I ever drove a wheat truck was 1956. No sooner had I returned from the grain fields of South Dakota than I received a letter informing me that a rural parish in Garfield County, Oklahoma, had lost its pastor and needed someone to preach there for the rest of the summer. My arsenal of sermons now stood at six or so, with most of them so thoroughly memorized I could have delivered them in total darkness.

August in an Oklahoma pulpit was a challenge. The heat always forced the windows open, and poor screening invited insects into every rural church. I arrived early that morning, before the heat of midday had turned the sanctuary of the little church into an inferno. I had borrowed a 1946 Chevy Sedan for the trip, having no car of my own. It was covered with red dust by the time I arrived in a too-heavy suit to deliver my rote, twelve-minute sermon.

Still, I had a sense of exhilaration the moment I walked into the fifty-year-old frame structure. The belfry, years before, had grown timber-weary, and the heavy bell had long since been removed. Apart from the renovated steeple, the carpentry structure was as charming as it had been the day it was dedicated in 1903, an incredible four years before statehood. The circular oak pews were dark and rich and held an American Gothic congregation of young and old. Some fifty souls came to church to worship that morning and to hear the first of my six twelve-minute, looking-glass sermons.

Their previous pastor could preach twelve minutes before breathing, and his marathon one-hour messages made my short sermons seem undedicated and anemic. His appeal, however, had not been as intense as his zeal. When my short sermon was finished, I was already a prime candidate for the pulpit. All six sermons which I owned could be preached, with memorized punctuation, in less than an hour and a half. The board of trustees offered me an annual salary of fifteen hundred dollars a year to "stay on," and I agreed to stay.

I bought a 1951 Chevrolet Coupe—clerical black—and a suit to match and commuted from college on weekends to the rural church to be a minister. In my naiveté I overrated my own importance to the rural community. But without question, the church became a priority for me. I loved the congregation passionately. My ardor was fixed on the joy of the older saints who were sick and infirm and shut off from others who would love and care for them. I discovered an immense number of lonely people—some the sons of the first settlers who had entered Oklahoma when it was Indian Territory. The good land and the strong people who cultivated it were suddenly mine. My land! My people! I wanted to be in their land and in their lives to do whatever I could for any who had need.

I was so in love with them that it took me a while to see you. It seemed to me that I was perfectly cut out to be a priest and not a parson. I could not imagine myself ever being able to prefer the love of one woman above the whole of all the men and women who comprised my red-shale bishopric.

Their faces long obscured your own: faces cut by hard winters and sun-blistered harvests, eyes wrinkled from decades of squinting over red landscapes. All the men wore overalls, and most of the robust women could drive John Deeres. They could also milk cows and diaper their infants with all the tenderness of the rough-chiseled Madonnas the land had ordained them to be.

You were among them, but never knew the music I found in hearing them sing their country hymns. Could you sense that I exulted to sit in a pulpit chair and see their faces, earnestly set in rural praise, with hymns that their parents had taught them in buckboards and farm wagons a generation before? The power of their celebration of God moved me. It was their celebration of themselves, their *gloria in excelsis* to a way of life that raised both churches and windmills on the plains. God knew I loved them!

I worked hard at my sermons, for it was a simple way to delight them, and their delight in any subject was my delight. I was never good at thundering against sin. Theologically, I knew they were sinners, but individually they were as good as the earth, which came without moral qualification. If the land was good, so were the people.

I learned your name three years before your significance to me began to dawn on my awareness. In fact, I had graduated from college and spent my first year in seminary before I gave myself the long-denied permission to ask you out. During those years, I sensed you were falling in love with me. It's fair to say that you loved first, and with such fervor that I could not deny you loved or honored this most powerful delusion within yourself. I heard you laughing in the vestibule of the church one day, and your laughter was so free that I knew you belonged to these wonderful rural saints. I saw you dressed in their same, simple clothes and set you free to become a part of them.

On our first date we went to dinner in the county seat. I remember how good I felt as we drove the red roads, leaving a cloud of dust behind us. It felt right to be together. We were cut from the same cloth. We were the grandchildren of those who had come into the county in the 1880s and 1890s. My forebears were born in Nebraska when the wagons were delayed coming into Oklahoma. Your grandmother had come to Oklahoma before the opening of the Cherokee strip homesteads, before the roads were cut. My grandfather had helped open the first railroads through the state. My romance with you was born in an intrigue—our mutual heritage and the people. But your love settled singularly upon me. It seemed too narrow a focus when there were vast and panoramic reasons to love.

It was here that I confess my ardor flagged. Younger five years than I was, you raced ahead of me to say we were in love. I declined so narrow and intimate a definition.

You told me that you loved me on our first date. I never liked the word *date*—it seemed a shallow word to define those portentous rendezvous that led to marriage. *Date*—that four-letter word that spoke of contrivances: arranged meetings so that love could get underway and people could make each other edgy with promises.

I did not consider your declaration of love to be spurious or immature. But what was *love* the way you used the word? Indeed, the way others used the word?

"To love" or be "in love" seemed glitzy but fickle. Certain movie stars fell "in love" and "out of love" again. One by one, my college acquaintances had fallen in love. With immature passion they spoke of the delirium of honeymoons and the ecstasy of their status.

I wasn't sure what "love" was, but I knew it would not work if only one of us claimed it. Still, it seemed sufficiently strong with you; I could not doubt that the word dominated your world view. Slowly and seriously you taught me there was a special substance in romance. You made me believe that it existed. I felt guilty for not being able to locate it in myself when it was so obvious in you. It was easy to see the stars in your eyes. But your eyes had obviously caught some glistening light that mine had missed.

Nonetheless, a marvelous idea caught hold of me. I had been loved twice by two women who spanned three generations, for my own mother was, indeed, beyond mid-life when I was born and your mother was barely old enough to be a mother when you were born. Twice loved by two women who were remarkably alike, and who for some odd reason had such affection for me as to see potential within my mediocrity.

A strange feeling of glory occupied me. The custody of my mother's affection released me eagerly to yours.

My mother never quit loving me, but she felt an excellence as though she was surrendering her life prize to the romantic, if untried, love you held. My own mother, made strong by life in the plains, insisted that *love* was a word with no right to itself until it had been tried in the laboratory of hardship. She defined her own love as systematic sacrifice, and as she surveyed you, she knew you held the same solid affirmations.

I wished that I felt the same love you felt and assured me was there. Such "falling in love" eluded me, and I could only stumble into liking. But your obvious affection won my confidence. There was born in me the strong desire to keep the treasure that you called love and freely offered unto me.

I loved your being in love with me and gambled with a trust. I believed this elusive substance you called love would become as definite for me as it was for you. It was on a January day in 1959 that I bought the ring and picked the cedar-lined lane by your old homestead as the place to give it to you. The occasion was perfect, you said. I trusted you for that as well. I would not let my uncertainties get in our way. You loved me and I felt good about it. All was well.

A SILENT HUNGER

My love must wait. Still, there's an appetite

That drives me to the tasting of that fruit

That never should be picked so green. The night

Stirs my desire and summons up a brute

That's always ravenous when he awakes.

No logic quiets him. No piety

Can make the bruin rest. His fire forsakes

All love and feeds on frothing chemistry.

How well you wait; avoid the hurried slur

Of love that can't forgo her meal one day.

Temperance alone waits best—prefers

The total soul, thus orders need away.

When love contrives the whole, then love is good.

And hurried need reduces love to food.

CHAPTER SIX
The Witness of the Cedars

You wore a diamond. The community approved of our engagement, and we saw the approval in various ways. The constable who made our completely safe streets safer grinned at us as we walked to church. The owner of the town's only café gave us pie after each meal we bought as a kind of gratis congratulation. The school board elected me to offer the invocation at your commencement. Wedding gifts poured in ahead of the event. The family doctor who delivered you into this world was proud to counsel you in every regard concerning those sexual matters that country people would not speak of for reasons of propriety.

Our romance was publicized beyond what I had expected or desired. The hoopla was overdone. I became ever more uneasy, still fearing that my own inconsistent definition of love and "falling in" or "being in" it had become no clearer.

The lane that formed the driveway to your home was lined with tall trees. Those cedars formed a canopy under which I had promised to marry you. The trees had a towering stability that made me feel short and indecisive. Each night as I took you home I shuddered inwardly, thinking of that night I would no longer take you to your home, but to mine. My home! I didn't have a home! And furthermore, if I somehow were able to build a nest from my modest income, providing for you was not so great a concern as being sure in my loving. I wanted for both of us all the fulfillment that our union would bring, but chastened my mind for daring to marry without the certainty of "in-love-ness." I hated myself for being so unsure about love.

The day approached.

Each year the chamber of commerce of our little town set forth the eligible young women of the hamlet in a penny-voting tradition by which one of them would be elected as the town queen. Even though we were engaged, your popularity in the community made it inevitable that you would be the town's choice.

On the night of your coronation, the small community was jubilant. You were the people's choice as you had been mine. I was proud, for even as your youthful, strapless-evening-gowned attendants scurried about you, everyone knew that you were promised to the young minister who, as part of the audience, surveyed the coronation.

I had dressed formally to match the occasion, and when the festivities were over, we drove home, still jubilant. Now, when I look at those old photos, I realize your "formal" was a style popular in that day, but uncommon and quaint in this. Still, that night a regal aura settled down upon you under the dainty rhinestone tiara. To view you on that occasion was to want to rush quickly into marriage—not because I was settled about the issue of love, but because I really wanted you.

My patience with being engaged was growing threadbare. But this was a proper community and things had to be done properly and in good time. The time was May—a proper time—printed in the engravings. I was the proper person, a proper bachelor who ministered in an acceptable way. The china they gave you was as proper as the white Bible they gave you to carry in the wedding. You were the proper bride, acceptable to the circle of fuss-budget women who gave you a bridal shower and loaded you with monogrammed sheets, towels, pillow slips, and silver, "His" and "Hers" embroidered on everything. I never understood why: we were not the type to fight over things that could have all been labeled "Ours" or "Theirs."

"It has to be done right," insisted the older women, who had guarded the social life of the church and community since the first houses had been built. Some of the ranchers were opposed to the things the farmers suggested. The musical *Oklahoma* had suggested that the ranchers and the farmers should be friends, but in the church they often found social reasons to disagree over propriety.

Elopement seemed increasingly more attractive, I decided. I grew impatient for the folderol to end, and ever more eager, therefore, to be married. The weeks crawled by. The wheat grew tall, as their light green heads beckoned us to walk in the fields. Nature had ever been the place for love. At weary last, the grain began to turn a lusty gold. Mid-May had come, and the sweet smell of harvest colored my senses and made me wish the last burdensome weeks of bachelorhood were out of the way.

On one particularly sunny afternoon we flew to the fields with a picnic basket and a Thermos of tea. I kissed you as we lay in the sun. Our kisses were but the gates of whatever walled and waiting experiences would come beyond the lagging ceremony. The same sun that had seen our grandparents come to the good land looked down on us that afternoon.

"The sun is good," I said.

"Do you love me with all your heart?" you asked.

"As I can know what love is," I replied.

You never pressed me for any contrived reply. You never demanded that I frame my feelings in your words. You simply, gratefully changed the subject. "Are you ready for the honeymoon?"

"Yes—after propriety," I complained.

We kissed and loaded all the paraphernalia back into the basket.

The week came to an end. Propriety grew to fervor. Friends arrived. The church was decorated with satin bows and long candles.

"We've had a lot of reverends since this county was settled and this church was built," said one of the women of the parish, "but you're the first to marry in it. I cleaned the windows and waxed the pews myself."

What was an honor to them was a horror to me. I remember that the night before the wedding, I drove you home. The bachelor's party had been an occasion of boredom and sweetmeats. But at least the months of waiting were over.

That night I opened your car door and let you out. The grain was early-ripened. The harvest moon came early through the gray-green boughs of the cedars. I kissed you for the final time before the ceremony, still wanting ahead of time what could only come when the time was proper.

"I love you," you said again, and you meant it.

I was quiet, treasuring your words without reply.

Winter Love

When first I saw the distant winter sun
Set gently free the auburn in your hair
With softer light, I knew I had begun
To understand the depth of our affair.
The country church in summer held our rite,
Some "legal" pledge that droned a legal love
I could not mean, until that crystal night
I stooped to kiss a snowflake from your glove.
It's strange December would confirm the vows
We made in May. Nor could I really know
The promise stood, till in the chill somehow
It came to me. I held you in the snow.
What summer but conceived, the cold allowed
To be, and winter-nourished love will grow.

CHAPTER SEVEN

Belated Affirmation

It was a May wedding. Country men in plain but sturdy suits brought their women. The congregation who had gathered in increasing numbers over my three years of ministry had swollen to a crowd such as the church had rarely seen. The waiting was over. Still the inner question lingered: What did it mean to be "in love"?

During our engagement, I had sifted my tentative logic again and again. I had managed the honesty of separating love into two facets: platonic and erotic. The platonic commitments were visible. I liked, of course, to appear proper in loving. I didn't want people to see me as romantically out of control. I wanted to appear "spiritually" in love. Eros was love too much in business for itself. Marriage commitment was structured and elitist in its ceremonial declaration. It was noble and clean and altruistic. I was a preacher and needed to be discreet. Still, I knew that beyond the high white altar waited the other kind of love—impatient, fiery, and immediate. Eros was the honeymoon, that kind of greedy intimacy which left its high-sounding pledges and made starving, "unspiritual" demands. Preachers should save their heavy breathing for their sermons. Altar love wore tuxedos and promised endurance regardless of health, wealth, or death. It eulogized by candlelight such things as character, idealism, God, the home, and eternity.

The problem was that both kinds of love were still too much one category for me. My thoughts mixed altruism and physical desire till they were tangled and twisted together. My noblest spiritual promises ended only in serving myself generous portions of indulgence. When I became really honest, desire loomed large over me. You wanted to give, "for better, for worse, for ever . . . in sickness and in health . . . till death do us part." On the other hand, I wanted the getting more than the giving.

I begged your forgiveness of my weaker egocentric definitions of love. I was unsure, and yet I craved the same certainty you displayed. I've heard it said that men crave sex yet call it love, while women idealize love beyond such hungry definitions. It seemed to me a remote proposition that Eros could ever bring me to that satisfying self-sacrifice I chirpingly promised at the altar.

In the weeks just prior to the wedding, a new issue began to occupy my mind: integrity—honor in search of the best reputation. If one could not know the surety of "being in love," one could at least tell the truth. The words of Richard Lovelace in *Lucasta, Going to the Wars* resurfaced in my memory: "I could not love thee dear so much, loved I not honor more."

I knew that if I ever had a chance to be "in love," it could only lie in the formal promises of the wedding, for those vows were based on integrity. Real love had to be built on honor and not appetite.

For millennia Jewish marriages have been made secure by this very principle. When Jewish people made altar promises, they kept them. They understood promises were made to be kept, especially altar promises. This principle made the child-marriage vows of the European feudal system sometimes result in happy marriages, and always result in stable marriages.

In the midst of my unresolved inner quarrels over the nature of love, the day finally came. The church was filled to overflowing by two o'clock. Everyone was on time except the parson. I stood there fidgeting, angry that the preacher, who was clearly a tardy, bumbling man of the cloth, had abandoned us. While I waited, one of the groomsmen, in an effort to ease my nerves, offered a kind of busy chitchat. He turned to me and said, "It must be wonderful to be in love."

"It must be," I replied. He detected the uncertainty.

"What? Are you not in love?" he asked. His tuxedo made him look more like my formal judge than my personal friend.

"I can't say for sure," I replied.

"If you don't know for sure that you are in love, you ought to march in there right now and call this whole thing off!"

I looked at the crowd in fear and felt weak at his terrifying suggestion. Anybody else would have agreed with him. The whole world married on the basis of falling in love. Still his logic seemed unsound to me.

"No," I said, "I will not call it off. I will, rather, stand there at the altar, where I have so often preached the truth, and once more speak in truth. Honor precedes love, and everything good is rooted in integrity." He looked puzzled that I could suddenly be such a practical philosopher in what to him seemed the shadow of the gallows. His jaw dropped open in unbelief. His long chin crushed his dickey and tie. My logic was clearly an unsure, unworthy way to him. In a while the parson arrived, and we spoke the formal words and made the legal promises, all with integrity, as I had planned.

The aisles soon filled with reception lines, and a gallery of photos was born in a thousand flash bulb explosions. It was over in a fatiguing four hours, and at last we climbed gratefully into our car and drove away on the honeymoon. How odd it felt suddenly to realize that I wasn't taking you home—at least to your home. From now on I would be taking you to mine. We were married. Love was defined. And I still felt like I was taking you on a date—a carnal, legal, long-lasting date. The strange sensation hit me that we were both very right and very wrong at the same time. We were doing things right and quite possibly doing the right thing. I thought of how many things were made possible just by saying "I do." I felt sheepish driving away from the church and thinking of all that we were now allowed to do because of our vows.

I still felt sheepish a couple of hours later when we arrived at the motel, a hundred miles away. I felt like I needed to show my I.D. so the clerk would understand. We checked in. The man behind the desk noticed our car outside with "Just Married" stenciled in shoe polish calligraphy. He gave us our room key and smiled oddly at me. It was clear he had said his "I dos" somewhere earlier. I wondered if he had really felt "in love." I had the oddest inclination to ask him about it but restrained myself. Still I wondered what right he felt he had to grin the way he did. I needed neither his permission nor his encouragement.

From that night, the months flew by. The fields yielded up their grain. Finally the sod itself was turned over to become furrowed fields ready for the new planting and thus the next harvest. We found, through an unusual channel of ministry, a new and interim position a long way from the rural church where we were married. We moved from Oklahoma to Iowa that winter. It was our first time to live outside of Oklahoma, and we discovered winter in a new way. More than just winter, we discovered the romance of winter. The snow came frequently and piled up in great walls along every road. By general agreement, that winter was the worst ever. Even the older Iowans said it had snowed more that winter than they could ever remember. They seemed a little miffed at God about it actually. But we were enchanted.

There was always a newness in the snow, and nothing so shuts out the world as the white silence that buries all commerce in formal sanctity. Most of those we knew avoided the storms, but we relished them. The best way to see a snowflake is on an eyelash. So what others watched through windowpanes we saw close at hand.

Walking in this magic white world, I suddenly felt alive. I was struck by a strange emotion, a new exhilaration. I watched a snowflake catch a curl of your auburn hair and stick in obstinacy. You laughed and the cold drew a clear, pure sound into your laughter.

"This is it!" I cried. "Now I love you—all at once!" I stopped and drew you up to me and we embraced in the falling glory. At once I knew who you were and who I was. I understood my own doctrine; honor does come ahead of sensate love. Integrity I had offered you on a May day in Oklahoma, and the unmistakable feeling of love had arrived at its own pace in the snowy enchantment of Iowa. As for me, I was the same, yet not the same. I was "in love," yet still "in honor." I knew that when honor precedes everything, everything is right. And in the rightness, love is free to find itself.

In the powerful exaltation of a new declaration, we stopped beneath a lonely lamp post. The flakes swirled furiously about us and shut the world away. "I love you," I said softly. The silence of the night folded us into oneness. I kissed you.

Heritage

A hundred years ago, in these high plains
My mother's mother came to be. And I,
Who never saw the winding wagon trains
She knew, at last beheld the endless sky
That was her cradle's canopy. We came
Much later, you and I, into the land
Our kinsmen knew. And there we found the same
Unspoiled force. This heritage was grand!
Heirs we were to prairies and the wind.
And leathered souls who broke sullen sod,
Year after year, to call the grain again—
Then reap the grain once more to honor God.
Here you conceived a child whose life was free
Whose heritage declined a century.

CHAPTER EIGHT
Nebraska

My seminary studies ended as did the interim position in the Iowa congregation. I was ready at last to become the pastor of my first "full-time church." The church I would serve was in a river town of eastern Nebraska. I remember how frightened we were. I was afraid the congregation wouldn't like me, though I was all but sure they would adore you. I remember my curious sense of destiny as I prepared to drive into the state for the first time. The state line was the meandering Missouri River, and I actually felt excited as we drove onto the bridge that spanned it.

My great-grandparents had barged their way across that very river in covered wagons before the bridge was built. My grandmother had been born in the plains west of the Missouri River on the trek west. Because she had been born in the brand-new state of Nebraska, her parents even named her Sadie Nebraska. I felt exhilarated to realize my grandmother had been born here a scant seventy years before me. Remembering their love for the frontier, I felt a strange sensation of homecoming. "Just think," I said, "the old Mormon trail passed right through here. Brigham Young's 'handcarters' crossed the river just north of here and wintered on the Omaha side of the river." You were untouched by my historical enthusiasm. As always, your practical side retreated from my naive excitement.

We drove across the silver-brown river. Beside the highway bridge was the old railroad trestle. Every rivet in the steel bridge was rusted, and the drab black iron was laced together with orange freckles that bled in rusty stripes.

It was a moment of sunlight and new beginnings. I felt strange genesis feelings. I drove across the river possessed by two loves. I loved Christ, in whose name I was coming to serve Nebraska. I loved you for your willingness to become one with those I would serve. Before the car droned to a stop, a gaudy cock pheasant displaying his summer colors, bolted into the red sky like a prairie comet. I was content.

"This is the land of William Jennings Bryan," I said.

And Willa Cather and Mari Sandoz," you added.

"The Union Pacific starts in Omaha," I said.

You asked where it ended. "At the ocean," I said, letting you know I had no idea. After all, it didn't matter where the railroad ended; it was enough to know that it began in Nebraska.

Though we had never been to the state before, we felt instantly at home. The parsonage came alive with activity. We unboxed our belongings. The house had not been built for us. Still, you took the small house and made it ours. There were raspberry bushes and fruit trees in the back and a respectably green lawn in the front. We weren't exactly homesteaders, but we were convinced that we belonged.

The congregation was small—a composition of warm folks who knew God and the land. There were few "old timers" in the congregation, and thus I felt much less romance than I wanted to feel. In fact, most of the younger members, like us, had also discovered the state by crossing the Missouri.

Before the end of our first month in the little river town, a square block in the business district caught fire and burned. The Historic Hotel was destroyed, and much of the city's quaint charm perished with it. Before the end of our first year, the thawing of spring snows changed the Missouri from a river into an ochre ocean; our small city became a brown Venice of angry, muddy waterways. Valuable farmland was destroyed along with many of the homes in our city. The floods at last receded. Summer came.

Our first vacation came in July.

We decided to drive west and see the rise in the plains and the great dome of the western skies. The night skies intrigued us most. We had never seen the stars as we came to know them in Nebraska. They defied their light-year definitions and seemed to hang just above the prairies.

Winter on the plains can be vicious, but Iowa had made us ready. We learned to love Nebraska's winters even more than her summers. The silence of a great white storm, the fireplaces and teakettles and hot bread, formed the ecstasy of our January communion. I reveled in Whittier's delightful prophecy:

The sun that brief December day
Rose cheerless over hills of gray,
And, darkly circled, gave at noon
A sadder light than waning moon.
Slow tracing down the thickening sky
Its mute and ominous prophecy—

And suddenly, we would be "Snow Bound."

When the storms were most furious, we most loved them. Robert W. Service in *The Spell of the Yukon* spoke for both of us when he wrote of December. He spoke of the white, silent winters, the "strong life that never knows harness." He exulted in Canada's winters, and we applied his songs to ourselves from January to January:

The winter! The brightness that blinds you,
The white land locked tight as a drum,
The cold fear that follows and finds you,
The silence that bludgeons you dumb.
The snows that are older than history,
The woods where the weird shadows slant;
The stillness, the moonlight, the mystery,
I've bade 'em good-bye—but I can't.

I had never believed that those who served Christ should "sanctify their geography." Only people are sacred and beloved of God, not places. God prefers no province above another. Yet, for me, God had given us this place, and the place was good.

I bought a shotgun that first year and learned to hunt. I was never a good hunter, though in time my skill improved. But hunting was nature, and nature was the prairies teeming with life. How I loved the russet fields studded with snow, and the sound of my own boots crunching across a sea of white, listening for the crow of a cock pheasant on a clean winter morning. The mackinaw I wore and the Thermos of hot coffee made me ever more certain that God had ordained this province for me. Here, where the Platte River meandered across the plains, frozen and still, I walked and rehearsed God's goodness. Long before me, my kinsmen had walked the wide, generous banks of this same frozen river.

I could see why the Hebrews first found God in the light of the stars and in the sighing wind. The field became for me His dwelling place. Not only did He pervade the streams and the fields, but He seemed present in the very lives of the people in our parish. They were the real dwelling place of the divine Savior, Who met with us each time we met with them.

Do you remember the old man whose face was raw-red from seventy winters on his farm? He and "his woman" were possessed of a life-force that came from breaking sod for half a century of springtimes in the plains. They had married in 1913, and he had followed a shining plowshare that cut a black furrow, fifty years long. For the first twenty-five years, he had followed his great Clydesdales, and for the last twenty-five, he had driven a gasoline tractor. And best of all, they were patient with my naiveté. They were alive with the resonance of living on the land, and their quiet dynamism surged through their quaint simplicity. They had seen the Almighty in a thousand prairie storms, yet listened patiently as I described God more weakly in my sermons.

How much they taught us about life on the plains. We learned how to use the autumn to store the fruit of summer. The old woman's gnarled hands were strong with the seriousness of her task. They dipped from the steaming cauldrons of glass jars a delicious security against the winter. We learned to eat in February what we canned in August.

The old man finally grew faint with cancer. We watched that firm frame that had never yielded to the harsh life of the plains, lose, at last, a wretched battle with his ugly inner enemy. I wanted so to help him win against this foe that out-fought him. I held the giant hand that once had managed the rough handles of a wooden plow. I prayed that the God whom he once absorbed from the brown earth of Nebraska through the very soles of his leather boots would heal him. It was no use. The enemy was too great. The old man died. I put my arm around his new widow, who, after sixty years of marriage, could only say that from Nebraska to heaven was not a long distance.

There were others like these two. Others whose passing left us all the more alone and yet fulfilled. The land was ours—as they were. I wanted to touch, feel, and belong to the land as they did. I wanted to see

Christ in a kind of primeval splendor, like sunrise in Eden. I never drove through the green plains at daybreak except that I said of the state, in the words of Eleanor Farjeon: "Morning has broken like the first morning." Or the first verse of the Te Deum Laudamus:

We praise thee, O God.
We acknowledge thee to be the Lord.
All the earth doth worship thee.

It was a good land—and good to us. In December of our first winter there, I placed my hand on you and felt the movement of new life. I knew the baby would come in the middle of the furious winter. But I also knew it would be all right. It had to be! Our love would have all that it could desire: the land, the people, ourselves, and a child—a son or daughter. The child would be born less than a hundred miles and a hundred years from where a nameless midwife had brought my own grandmother into the world. We were home. I touched you again. Our unborn baby moved beneath my hand and you smiled.

THE CUBS

The cubs are come! The den is home. See how
They romp. Their noise is contribution to
Our simple joy this present hour. For now
They're cubs. And now we celebrate the two
Of them that are of us. The summer's fair,
The woods are warm with sun. Dance, little ones.
And play for us to warm our little lair
Before the forest hides from distant suns.
What shall the future hold for you? What pain
May come with autumn's frost? The woods may grow
Quite barren and all the sunny fields know rain.
Your play could know the killing blight of snow.
Play in the sun, for no day comes again,
Time feeds on boys and leaves them merely men.

CHAPTER NINE

The Cubs

They came to us from God and from our promises to each other. Before they came, the waiting came: the swelling of your womanhood, the grand grotesqueness, the obtuse excellence. We cheered impatiently and waited twice. Like others we observed around us in the church, we feared the lagging days would disappoint us. We trembled lest our children should come as things in horror. Twice our fears proved groundless.

Our daughter arrived in February, and our son on a balmy night in summer a year and a half later. They were born a little close together, and their closeness made them later seem like twins. The care that they required left us sometimes tired in the unceasing demands of their infancy. But they grew. Before long, they were alive with themselves, and the world they discovered was filled with sunshine and snow, created just for them.

The days seemed to tumble over each other as they played, like young cubs in a Disney nature film. Our love, endorsed by our delight, was quite unwilling to see them suffer because of any unsteadiness in our relationship. We came to understand that their security was born in our togetherness.

Our youngest especially needed us. He suffered several seasons of pneumonia in his infancy, and each attack left him weak. We were always afraid that his convalescence would be too slow to allow him to regain the stamina he needed before his next attack of illness came.

But when his first winter was gone, he seemed well enough, and we decided we would take the children camping. We were never good campers, and yet our parish paid us such a small salary that other kinds of vacations were unaffordable.

How nice it was, and how splendid the mountains were. I remember how you cheerfully warmed the children's milk by the open fire that blazed before the little tent we had borrowed for the outing. We traveled in the Rockies, which were only a few hundred miles from home and which provided us with new vistas for our relationship.

Camping intimidated us at first. We were afraid that bears would rob our picnic baskets. It was an unfounded phobia that gave way to the more real danger that our own cubs would steal all they could nibble while our backs were turned! I remember the simple joy of the four of us zipped into one large sleeping bag. We were lovers—a family of lovers. Our combined togetherness with the children was sleeping-bag cozy, and our little ones added to the warm completion of ourselves.

They grew. Every year before they started to school, they welcomed our annual trip to the mountains as did we. I remember all my mother had taught me of real abundance, and now I tried to teach it to them. We continually let them know how rich we all were. They were so well off that they never seemed to notice how we bypassed the swank motels, opting for life under the blue sky and borrowed canvas.

Ours was a wealthy poverty that taught us first to love long walks on shaded trails. And the children, too, enjoyed the sun and the trees. I remember a night in Wyoming, when we were snuggled into fleecy sleeping bags. We turned on the radio just before falling asleep and heard a static and nasal, electronic voice tell us that some bears had mauled a family of campers in Wyoming that very afternoon. We suddenly became afraid. We were terrorized by an image of a vicious animal ripping its way into our tent.

We looked at each other and then at our own cubs. We spoke in whispers as to what course of action we should take if real bears came. I went to the car and took out our camping ax. I felt nervous and looked at the ax doubtfully. I wondered how either of us would really fare at axing bears. The darkness closed in tightly when I extinguished the battery lantern. We listened for a crashing and lumbering form among the timbers. Gradually the hours passed, and the fresh light of morning seemed to wake the alien forest with a new friendliness. Our fatigue overcame us and our taut bodies eased into rest. We dozed just as the sun was becoming intense. The children stirred, awake all at once. That is how they always woke up—suddenly clamoring for play clothes and tennis shoes and a chance to run.

Happily, as I look back, I see that most of the time our protective instinct was not trapped in dread such as axing bears would require. Still, the children's welfare made the days anxious. The little one always had a fever, and the older, a special reason for concern. Both of them, once or twice, required minor hospitalizations and extra care.

There were simple things that kept their common necessity in mind. Once we lost our son at Disneyland. And our daughter once suffered an injury and a concussion that was to require a long hospitalization and a siege of plastic surgery to correct.

But in the process of their growing, we learned and grew, too. During their teen years, our means improved. We learned how close a family could grow while traveling in a small European car across the Swiss Alps or the Rhine Valley or the rolling hills of Cornwall. In foreign climates, we were forced to use good, simple English and to talk to each other as we traveled. Our rented auto became a womb of forced communication. We talked to each other in those lands where we knew too little of the local tongue to talk to anyone else.

I loved you as you loved the children and myself. I loved you for being unafraid to drive those left-handed cars on the highways of England. I loved you because you made the children secure when they felt menaced and alone in Mexico. I loved you for chiding me when I was too protective of them both. I remember the uneasiness that you quieted so that I could watch our son race to the top of the Teotihuacan Pyramids. Best of all, I remember how calm you were in every crisis. I was often tense with anxiety until I knew they were safe and the crisis was over.

The days ran past each other, and at last the cubs were taller than us. "Sunrise, sunset, swiftly flow the years . . ." And soon we all were older and yet made one by the fleeting years. There is a joyful sadness in those years we see now in the photo album. But yesterdays are wistful only because they cannot be called back. We're glad their footprints grew. We knew one day that we would watch them step across the threshold for the last time. The door would swing outward and then shut, echoing with reverberations only our ears would hear. They would have left the nest, and we would have to watch them make their way in the world they had seemed to fear as much as we once feared. Then we would test how well we had parented and how thoroughly they had learned the lessons we had taught.

Debt

I love you, church. You wear an empty face,

Yet His and yours are one. If love can be,

Here's what I give to you. Here are the ways

I love. I love you as He loved the sea

Whereon He walked—as eagles love the sky.

I love you with an eager joy born twice

Or as a goodly merchant who would buy

Though it cost all—the pearl of greatest price.

I love you as a prisoner set free.

I love you as a treasure in a field.

I love you as I prize Gethsemane,

Where brother-love bled rich and hate was sealed.

As steel can maul a hand—and make men new—

I have been loved and therefore I love you.

CHAPTER TEN

A Wider Love

A fter five years, we resigned from our first church and moved into Omaha to begin a new church. Our new work was in the only large city that Nebraska knew. To begin a congregation demands a great deal. It required so much time that much of the romance we had time for in the smaller church was lost.

The congregation grew, and its very demands seemed to rise against our relationship. A decade of years proclaimed a growing agenda. We had once claimed Nebraska like conquistadors, but were all too soon discovering that her beautiful people had turned from being our possessed to being our possessors. Unlike the rural church, the city church grew so rapidly that its few members soon numbered more than two thousand, and still they came.

It was not until we got to the city that I struggled more with the problem of pain in the ministry. Why it should have begun then, I cannot say. Perhaps I walked more in the country and took more time to know the outdoors Christ, who was complete in Himself in nature. Perhaps my own process of aging made me suddenly aware of those who had to face great ordeals of suffering in which the God of mercy seemed so often deaf to their needs.

Even if we had no real answer for pain, at least we had compassion. The city church became a haven for the hurting, and we both sought ways to extend the sovereignty of the Savior until He who had caused us to love each other should extend His love to others through us. As the smaller church had its special reminiscences, so did the large one.

We both loved Anne, whose charm and wit had made her instantly the sweetheart of the church. Then came cancer. Anne turned to us, and we turned to Him. Eagerly we besought Him to help her win her battle with that disease that all her charm and wit could not forestall.

Her dying hurt us because we could not stanch the pain that it caused her. It wasn't just that we lost a friend to death, but that her dying so dehumanized her, that she lost her personhood long before she died. It was hard indeed for us to understand the horror of what had happened to Anne. Why did God allow such a brilliant woman to become the sallow, empty-eyed thing that now lived in the place her bright personality had once held sway?

Anne was but one.

There was also Bill, a tall Nebraskan, whose excitement in life was blunted by a dull prophecy from his doctor. He, too, died in tubes, strung up in the rubberized paraphernalia that prolonged only his physiology, not his life.

I was with him when he died, and he made me promise to care for his widow until she could find work, for the disease had claimed their livelihood and left their family penniless.

I made promises to him . . . to them . . . to all. Each of them needed my time. Funerals were not so frequent in the city church, for most of the families were young. But the helpless loneliness of those who had to watch as death invaded their families grieved me and demanded more and more of my stamina.

I found that no serious issue could be answered quickly. I remember the horror of Bucky's death, killed by a speeding car. Here I wrangled once again with God. Why was a little boy in our congregation impaled on the spike of a Buick hood ornament? Bucky's family took months for the healing. So did Ricky's parents. Ricky was another child with a congenital heart ailment that claimed his life on the operating table. More and more, people seemed to bring us problems we could not pray away.

They loved us as much as they seemed to need us. Perhaps they loved us because they needed us. Here was a part of our difficulty with the parish. You felt they needed me, and I felt they needed us. It was your continuing sense of prayer as a way of life that was the motivation for my life of prayer.

I never loved you more than when you shared our personal time with those we served. There were times when I knew you resented the congregation for moving in on our lives. How many hundreds of calls interrupted those very special meals that you had labored so hard to prepare? You knew that the preparation would delight me. Yet the meals grew cold and their delicacy faded on the plates when our evenings together were obliterated by people's urgent pleas.

We have always reacted differently to need. I rarely found tears my best response. I confess that crying never seemed a manly quality, but sometimes my maudlin moods took control of my emotions. By contrast, you were a strong example of emotional consistency. You laughed more readily and freely than I.

Naturally the congregation loved you, but I could tell in your strong silence that you often felt incidental in our marriage because of their needs, which more and more came between us.

I could see what they were doing to us, but I found myself unable to stop loving them, even as I would have been unable to stop loving you. You were my dearest love, but I could not forsake all I felt for them. My ardor for both you and them was hidden in a principle that had grown with me across the years. I knew Christ loved them all, and I was not at liberty to despise anyone that He loved. It was in no sense a negative principle, however. I loved because He loved—not as intensely, but just as certainly.

When I would see you caught in the fatigue of the endless stream of people who came through our home, I loved you for a second reason: your generous offering of yourself to these needy Nebraskans. There was ever a note of cheer in your demeanor. The tea was always hot, and the lemon near at hand. The best thing about your hospitality was that it was generous and instant. You were a woman whose love was visible in all your hand extended.

Eyes welcome friends before words do, and no one who ever saw your eyes could doubt that you loved life. Thus, we were one in all we loved. How safe romance is when Christ's love precedes it. There were times when you might have been impatient or short with me, but you served all those I served. I wanted not to love them sometimes, for they stole our lives with their urgent issues and all too often took the time we craved for ourselves.

I remember a horrible Friday when I had a funeral in the afternoon and a wedding rehearsal in the evening. The next morning was a second funeral with an afternoon wedding. I remember the emotional portages that swept me between grief and joy as event followed hard upon dissimilar event. One hour I was ministering to those in despair—the next hour was characterized by bright hope.

I can think of specific people who have taken my time and, thus, yours. None required more time than a very talented dyslexic man who had never learned to read. I wanted to teach him. I began to meet with him regularly and to introduce him to letters and words. Week by week, my frustrations increased as my reluctant disciple learned slowly the simple glory of English. I used to think in my restlessness, *Why doesn't he learn faster so I can get home to you earlier?*

I felt like Professor Higgins in *Pygmalion*. How hard it was to hurry a grown man to syllable recognition. For one year, I taught my friend—we moved from simple children's classics to the New Testament—and by the end of the year, he had learned to read. But you and I were one year older and our lost year was unrenewable.

I am sorry that I did not handle church urgencies in a more balanced fashion. I loved you both: the church was His body, and you, the very extension of myself. I was unable to resist or renounce either. But how could I affirm both lovers and yet keep the ardor of both of my affairs?

How often from Valentine's Day to Valentine's Day did we celebrate our love by reading Elizabeth Barrett Browning's *Sonnets from the Portuguese*. Her Sonnet 43 was our favorite:

How do I love thee? Let me count the ways.
I love thee to the depth and breadth and height
My soul can reach, when feeling out of sight
For ends of Being and ideal Grace.

And we found our own maturing confession in her final lines:

I love thee with the breath,
Smiles, tears, of all my life!—and, if God choose,
I shall but love thee better after death.

She had spoken for us both. And here at last, loved deeply, I also loved beyond the boundaries of our relationship and was delighted that you understood. In loving all those whom Christ called me to love, you sometimes waited in the wings. Christ had called us both to love more widely than ourselves.

REPENTANCE

I sipped the cream of our relationship

And glutted on your generosity.

I grasped your bounty—seized with a strangle grip

Your free and ever soft gentility.

You called—my ears heard voices far away.

Your face was ever there—I passed it by

And gazed at other faces in the fray.

I loved the distant and the near denied.

What arrogance that public altar vows

Should be so showy when they say, "I do,"

Flashing diamond rings before a crowd

Of exhibitionists, who never knew

That public words speak for their own applause

And make us strut before our poor hurrahs.

CHAPTER ELEVEN
Repentance

When lovers ask forgiveness, their repentance is often a rare and haunting brokenness.

Mary Magdalene sinned openly and almost answered for her deeds with public execution. But marital transgressions are seldom blatant; they suffer only quiet guilt before the stern but mute tribunals of the soul.

Marriages rarely die in blazing flames of infidelity. They die from lack of care. I always promised myself I would not take for granted that which I prized so dearly.

I never wronged you in great ways. My sins were little transgressions. But each became a thin filament in a growing web of stress. And each of them was committed always in the name of ministry to someone else in need. You served the church by gently forgiving me for all the promises I made to you and later broke on their behalf. I first sinned by accepting your ready forgiveness and later by expecting it.

If I needed to be five minutes late for dinner, I knew you wouldn't question it. If I were caught stealing time from you to give to the congregation, I knew you wouldn't mind. I came home so often fatigued from caring for those outside of the parsonage, that I was too tired to care for those inside of it.

Then there were the grand hurts. In the ninth year of our marriage, your mother died. You were forced to watch her atrophy in the pain of an incurable degeneration. She required so much of your love, and yet I confess now my own lack of support. I had cared for so many with cancer in the church that my eyes were blinded to your need by my own familiarity with death. A thousand times I have wished I could turn back the clock and touch you when your bright eyes were made dead by fear and fatigue. I lived with you without shedding a single tear to let you know that you did not grieve alone. How shall I say I'm sorry?

The years were far too furious for me to count, and losing count, I ran too fast. From New Year's Eve to New Year's Eve, we gathered at the clock. We toasted the loud chimes that signaled the hassled pace of the new year. We lived that year never catching the import of its unending demands. I had set goals for myself designed to push my own career along. I wrote and published, and all I wrote, you typed a thousand times—never of necessity, but with joy.

I am lost to remember all the brutal nights that I drove us to the finishing of some manuscript. In the wee small hours of morning, while the children slept, we spoke in the darkness, of my career, of some deadline, or another hurried goal. Yet never did you castigate me for the dreams I wanted to achieve.

How glorious was your celebration of my life! Your love served the typing table as a kind of altar where you were a high priestess in love with me and all my dreams. You never have been a good editor of my work. Your weakness was your lack of critical judgment—you loved all I did and grew angry with my critics, even when they were right. You loved me with that faith that believed you would one day be married to a real writer. How did you justify keeping your faith fettered to me? Did you even consider the price it cost your hope of your own career just to believe in me so much?

I think not.

For you were angrier than I when a rejected manuscript came back again.

I wondered that you never wanted life a little more for yourself. I remember reading you a passage by a certain woman psychologist who felt that women of real stature should have their own goals and not identify too closely with the goals and dreams of their husbands. She called the serving wife a "limited success woman." It seemed a slur from which I wanted to deliver you. Yet the statement indicted me more than you. At such moments of truth, I confessed my selfishness to God and to you. But you insisted that my life and yours were exactly what you wanted for yourself.

For a long time, the idea distressed me. I tried to get you to seek your own career—to take up some diversion or hobby or social circle with other women. Still you desired to lose your ambition in the service of my own. The more I encouraged you to seek your own career, the more you moved into mine. Such wholesale endorsement of my dreams made it easy to take advantage of you. Without realizing it, I began to take the willful submergence of your own needs into my life as normal to a marriage relationship.

For fifteen years, you worked as a secretary in the city because without your salary we could not survive. Our first church was too small to pay us anything more than subsistence. Yet your salary was never a contested contribution to our funds. It was always as much mine as yours. It was not that I tore it from you; you always gave it to me without the slightest possessiveness. I took it for "our" account.

Here was another of my blunders. You were content in every state of substance or need. What funds we had were enough for you. I was the materialist—the malcontent—particularly in early marriage. I seemed to need so much more than you. Without grumbling, you seemed to fancy what I fancied, to crave exactly what I craved, to need what I needed.

How you scrimped from this or that to be sure that the groceries were adequate or that the children had mittens in the winter. The car had to run so I could serve the people. Against the grocery fund or the clothing fund, I waged a practical war. Spark plugs for the car seemed more important to me than mittens or galoshes for the children.

What bothers me now, as I reconsider these years, is that I felt my priorities were *the* priorities.

But it was not only the material crisis I resented.

How I wish I could have given more than I did of myself. My stamina ever seemed greater than yours. I required less sleep and could hurry the days and yet warm the long hours of night with the bulb in my desk lamp. Every day was pushed by a thousand different ideas to yield up every minute for my goals. Every season of the year was made to serve. This was especially true of winter. While the snow stacked silently outside my study window, I read on into the night . . .

night after night. Perhaps this extra reading time was why I always loved winter best of all. But while I steeped my mind in the winter storms, you were always down the hall typing until your stamina was spent. Two or three A.M. would come upon us like married celibates pushing the wee small hours for more product. When the children cried, the clatter of your typewriter would stop while you marched off to their bedroom to be a mother. When they were quiet, zombielike, you came back again. But best of all were those times I heard your footfalls on the oak floor coming in my direction. You would slip in, set a cup of steaming tea by my lamp, slip your arms around me and kiss me—a phantom Eros in the driven night.

Why was I so serious? Why could I not more often stop to enjoy your youth? Mechanistically I would greet your query of love by asking how some manuscript was going. You would kiss me, reply, and ask me where to hyphenate something like "Trinitarian" before returning to your work, leaving me to mine. Sometimes we saw the glory of the seasons. In early marriage, we walked regularly in the snow, but even then we hurried the winters as we grew older.

I regret those lost Februarys. If I could, I would repeat them and make each one better serve your sense of self-importance. I would give each church member my fatigue and answer you with freshness.

Others would receive the lackluster stamina that was left over after I gave you the day's vitality.

My eye would be brighter for you. My ear would never grow dull of hearing of your special needs. I would exalt the low, low altar of your requirements. I would give each day's best hours more sparingly to those who barged into our togetherness. My hurried pace would slow itself when I walked past your chair. The eager seasons would be much more our own— could I come again to younger love.

In this dark night

In this dark night of turbulence and fear

Across the aching gulf we long to touch

Each other's wounds and make our healing such

That somehow joy might grow from barren cheer.

I feel as though I've wounded you in soul

And amputated what I deeply prize,

Made jumbled order, jangled silence rise

To threaten us with life out of control.

You, too, must hurt to see the circumstance

Of furious events laid at my feet

So that no logic ever could explain

The deeds against my keep. May diamonds dance

Alive the deadness of our eyes and cheat

The hate that tries to slash our love with pain.

CHAPTER TWELVE

The Season of Darkness

We were married for a dozen years before our first real trial by fire. It was our sixth year in the city. It pains me even now to recall that winter of our discontent.

It was our year of greatest crisis, and yet the year brought me to an open confession of my need for both you and Christ. It was for me a season of double pain, for I was made to look upon a twin Medusa.

The first trial was a material matter that came in the form of a congregational recommendation that I be dismissed as pastor of the church. The charge was from some older members who felt my leadership was too erratic and impulsive for older folk to follow. My worst fears had to do with finances. I was ill-trained for any other vocation. I knew how to "work for God," as we said in seminary, but I had never held secular employment for any length of time. I sought frantically to find another pulpit, but none was open and fears of being unable to provide for my family tormented me. For months, the all-powerful chairman of the council continuously pressured me to resign. Most of the others on the council of the church agreed with him. When the critical vote came, I was saved from this pressure by the congregation itself. The majority of those to whom I ministered stood firmly against the council. I was in the unenviable position of living with a congregation who desired and courageously demanded that I continue, while the chairman of the board demanded otherwise.

I had never believed that God saw churches in terms of big and little people. How grateful I was that I had ministered to the "little people" who stood by us through these agonizing months of conflict, and were finally able to prevail.

The strain of trying to lead a congregation whose most prominent members did not want me to be the pastor often grew unbearable. I lost much of the joy that I had always felt about my calling. I could, here and there, see little reasons to rejoice, but my inner life grew bleak. Shakespeare's truth characterized my drab view of the whole gloomy time:

For we which now behold these present days
Have eyes to wonder, but lack tongues to praise.

Month after month, my tension with the council endured. Finally, beyond the agony of the church quarrel came the ultimate healing.

There was another Medusa I found I could not so easily look upon. To serve Christ is to opt for a kind of social separation that leaves a "man of God" set apart from the more ordinary folks of this world. He who serves God finds that he always walks with people, yet is alone. The problems can be great, and circumstances can become so furious that they call for steel psyches and a firm pier in the midst of turbulence.

I took the pastorate of the suburban church at the same time and age that a colleague took the pulpit in a neighboring community. Soon after we became pastors and friends, he lost his eyesight. His agony sent him into a maelstrom of despair. He purchased a red-tipped cane and went on trying to minister in a dark world. He tried to thrust his own handicap aside by radically giving himself to others. Our friendship deepened. His need was physical and mine was spiritual. Often I would read to him. His interest in the books I read would send us spiraling away into other fields of discussion.

His blindness set him on a pilgrimage from hostility to acquiescence, and finally to a second sight. Only then did he learn to revel in his visionary darkness. His sightlessness revealed a furtive independence. He was eager to reject help and strike out on his own to measure Milton's world of a paradise lost and regained.

In the year of my greatest despair, he shared with me the inner light which had come to him. "Never love people supremely," he advised me. "Love God before you love His people," he counseled. "For years I served the people of God. I loved the church of God, adored the things of God, but never God Himself. Now I love only God."

How bright his vision had grown in darkness!

At last I understand why Jesus condemned hypocrisy. It is the enemy of integrity. And every foe of integrity is also the enemy of trust. If those who are filled with "God-talk" can be evil, then all trust is elusive. When hypocrisy is widespread, saints themselves may be doubted. In such hypocrisy the very world is spoiled. Religion becomes a gray affair that only dresses white.

When my entire ministry was being questioned by the chairman of the council, I discovered that a man may appear to speak for God without sensing any obligation to love others. His popularity seemed impossible in light of his hypocrisy.

I felt much like young Goodman Brown in a story by Nathaniel Hawthorne. On his way back from the black mass, having seen the archdeacon of Christ burning black candles at a witches' coven, Goodman Brown could never trust his peers again. The first visitor in Gethsemane is always Judas.

Gethsemanes!

William Styron, in *Set This House on Fire,* sees the character Peter Leverett as a man haunted by dreams of betrayal. In one such dream, Leverett looks out his rain-streaked window and sees the form of a fiend slinking toward him—as menacing as hell itself. The harassed hero goes to the phone and dials his one true friend from whom, above all others, he could expect help. The phone goes unanswered, ring after ring, till finally the fiend is at his very glass. Then is born the real horror: through the streaming window pane, he sees that the fanged face is that of the one true friend he was trying to call for help.

Betrayed!

During those days I often named God the culprit of my lost trust. How often during my despair I turned toward you for the final source of strength, knowing without you I had no real support.

The months dragged by. The snow melted. And spring began to thaw the leafless winter. You met my crisis and gradually turned me from myself. Little by little, my preoccupation with depression subsided, and I came slowly to a newer faith that there was an answer. That reply lay in my restored confidence in both God and people. Trust was possible and believing had to be a part of a healthy future.

Before the crisis, I had been busy and full of "good works." Now I was in need, and I turned in that need to you. Once again I wondered if I had ever loved you or God. I despised the whole idea of serving either of you as the last resort. I was broken because my self-sufficiency was gone. I suffered all the more because I never admired those who turned to God only in a crisis.

Humility is often the gift of desperation. I had never been able to be alone with both of you at the same time. When I was deep in prayer or loving Him, I rather tended to be alone with Him. Later, as I emerged from this intensive religiosity, I wanted to be with you. But this crisis enabled me at last to integrate both of my loves. I made a vow that I would never again walk with you and God one at a time. We would—the three of us—live life openly in each other's presence.

It's odd that in the midst of hurried circumstance, one day may break in blue, then darken and shatter into night. I never will forget the agony of a Sunday in May that ended in our mutual disconsolation for each other's hurt. The chairman of the church council had finally become open in his hatred of me and demanded that my resignation be given at once.

The heavy demand of our adversary brought a thousand feelings of insecurity about our future. I never will forget your downcast look! His hate had fallen upon us openly and in public. The utter absurdity of his charges that I was inept in my leadership and ability to handle the problems of a growing church had left us unable to reply. I felt ashamed to be accused of poor administration. This accusation implied that I was guilty of something even worse, for he failed to define all that he meant by "poor administration," and it sounded as though he meant embezzlement or some great misuse of church property.

I remember the way your dignity seemed to give you precedence over our accuser. I saw your brown eyes blinded by a sting of having to answer vague congregational charges where their shouts came too furiously to hear their reason. I tried to argue for you, but my logic was cut off by my own unreasonable anger. When hate screams loudest, love's best answers are dulled to incoherence.

The afternoon of the congregational meeting gave way to one of the darkest nights our marriage would ever know. We both wept! I decided that I would no longer try to fight my enemies. They were too many. I sat up trying to compose my resignation, determined that when the next night fell, we would both be free of a church that did not seem to want me to be the pastor.

We joined hands and knelt beside our bed, just as you had taught the children to do. In some ways, we were children, imploring the Father in heaven to hear us. We prayed, I cannot say how long. Sometimes in our agony of hurt, we would stop and love, and our embrace, though awkward, seemed to say to our Almighty Audience that we intended to love each other and to endure together what must be lived out.

We were children, who prayed for our children. They were asleep in their bedrooms, trusting us to care for them. Did they doubt that our love for them would be able to provide the security they needed to survive the tempest? Did they even know that our day had been torn apart with an anguish that seemed to be everlasting? They believed in us, and we believed in God. Yet He seemed so remote in the awful, aching darkness.

That darkness was empty. But empty or not, it was friendly. We could touch each other whether or not we touched the Almighty. The darkness made it easier to talk. Sometimes we quit talking to God and just talked to each other.

The content of our love suddenly overwhelmed me. We kissed from where we yet knelt beside our bed. Then I drew you to the floor and we lay in the darkness, which had now filled itself with a divine presence.

"Now I know what Bob meant!" I cried into the darkness.

"Bob?" you asked, trying to grasp the rapid turn of the conversation.

"My blind friend. When he first became blind, he told me that in his darkness he learned that we too much love the things of God and too little love God Himself." I saw the error of my all-too-shallow affection.

I got up in the night and went to my study and scratched out my resignation. A few words were enough. No charges were answered; no excuses were rendered; no one was hurt; nothing was attacked. I thanked the church for its kindness and apologized to those who had found my ministry inadequate.

Sunday morning I arrived at the church early. I called a friend of mine in a distant city and informed him of the tangled situation that was forcing me to resign that very morning.

He was stunned.

"Perhaps you should resign," he said. "Still, your life speaks clearly of Christ. If you leave the church now, flying before the charges brought against you, you will remember only the pain of separation. Too many good things have happened. Why don't you tell them how you feel and that you are not resigning because you really want to, but because you do not want to embarrass them. Tell them you would rather not be judged by one man and his council, but by the whole church. For years you have tried to preach what it means to be the people of Christ. Now put your life and word to the test! If you have an authentic work of Christ, then it is time to ask them point-blank to demonstrate the love and mercy that you have exalted. It is not a church at all if it knows so little of mercy.

Suddenly it occurred to me that perhaps the congregation *was* on our side. In fact, there was a distinct possibility that most of the church council was on our side as well. How did I know whether or not the council really agreed with its autocratic chairman?

In the agony of trying to decide whether or not to resign, I called a special meeting of the council that afternoon. I appealed for real evidence that I had been a poor administrator.

We were at an impasse. The atmosphere was lava-hot. Realizing how little Christ's love was being shown by anyone, I asked for adjournment. But before they agreed to adjourn, a cry of support began to rise from those in attendance. The support began cautiously; soon it became a roar. They were all on their feet, unanimous—except for one. The agreement was glorious. My character now needed no endorsement by the hostile chairman.

In a furious instant, the storm passed. The sun shone more brightly than ever. I was not only acquitted, but I was celebrated.

The inglorious season had ended.

Maundy Thursday had turned again toward Palm Sunday. The chairman of the board had been soundly defeated. We were alive. More than that, we were set free to live in a love we would never again have to doubt. We knew now we could live without needing anything but Christ and each other.

Two Diamonds Two Decades Apart

The frost hung there—do you remember how
The January air stung your young face?
With all the warmth the wind chill would allow,
I kissed you by the cedars. The embrace
Was all I needed to confirm the vow.
I slipped the cold small ring inside your glove.
The tiny frozen stone said, "Wait, for now."
My promise glistened on the seal of love.
The years fled by and stole our youth. We heard
Our children cry—beheld our parents die.
Where have the flowers gone? Was it absurd
To let the frozen decades pass us by?
For twenty winters I have loved you so.
I long to find you diamonds in the snow.

CHAPTER THIRTEEN

The Twentieth Winter

Winter is our special time, and as each one rolls around it summons up again that distant season of our engagement. In our twentieth winter we had rented a car in Toronto and driven to Niagara Falls. The night held, as Shakespeare said, "an eager and a biting air." The impetuous, green Niagara River fell from Erie to Ontario. We stood at the rail to watch its hurried fall.

How can you force two days, twenty years apart, to stand together? Here we were, traveling to Niagara in our early forties to celebrate an event born two decades earlier on a cold Oklahoma day. On the Queen Elizabeth Way we drove a 1979 Pontiac, but on that earlier day we had driven a 1951 Chevrolet. I first gave you a ring and made you a promise, and you accepted both in the winter of 1959. Now, twenty years later, I had concealed a second diamond in the pocket of my mackinaw. This newer ring I saw as a way of uniting our current lives with old promises. I wanted the later and smaller diamond to bear witness to the first. As we were older, so were the promises of 1959. Of course, we had known winters of discontent, but they had yielded joyously in time to better seasons.

Life had become a celebration. I tried to lay your younger face above your present visage. The mask was somehow undersize—we were bigger for our years. Nothing of your inner light had diminished; your eyes were much brighter, your smile more free.

The water roared. It was winter, yet the gulls were there. They screamed and turned and rose. I knew that afternoon that every promise was important. I could see the fickle waters in their northward hurry. They ran and swirled toward Quebec as though Canada would give them a freedom they had not found in the United States. How well they matched the impetuous, restless search of our early marriage. Their unsteady turbulence seemed to long for their merger with a calmer sea.

In 1959, I had slipped the ring on your finger and said, "For better or for worse . . . I will always love you, cherish, and honor you." I had meant the vow, but I had not lived up to it well. Who makes a promise to cherish and always cherishes? Who pledges love and always loves? Yes, a thousand times in those past years I had not been as loving as I had promised; a thousand, thousand times I had not cherished or esteemed you. But our marriage held because all promises hold their own integrity. Though we who pledge are weak, the promises secure our wavering intentions.

Twenty years before, I had made the same kind of promises to God. I told Him He could have my life and I would forever serve Him. Yet I had vacillated between my pledge to Him and my own self-will. I ever gave and snatched back my commitment to Christ. Yet He must have known that the intent of my life was to serve Him, even when I acted in my own interest. And like Him, you received my pledge and discovered that I was not always loving, honoring, and cherishing. Still, our conflicts dissolved in those old promises.

The falls were deserted, and we were gloriously alone. We were triumphant. We had outwitted the crowds! What madness made most people come in the sultry summer? We had been to Niagara only once in summer and found it mired in tourism. Winter was for us a perfect time for setting the decades straight. We watched the water, and then I turned and slipped the glove from your hand. I placed a second ring on your finger, and looked at it in the cold mist until the frost forced you to replace your glove. We walked along the rail, then turned back to our hotel. We could not bring the years together, really. The decades still stood far apart. We were older, but the years were worth the aging. We knew now what we could not have known twenty years before: Love is not worthy of the name unless it can endure the test of twenty winters. A great deal of pain had passed beneath our faces. What would life be like when future decades passed? The winters would mark each anniversary and set us free to remember that the weather is never unfriendly. The snow but whitens the hair and thins the skin. And every value grows more dear and improves with age. The hearth is warmer in the shorter winters of our later, better years.

Winter knows no requiems—it ever celebrates the spring. It tends to freeze the memory as it awakens the world to hope. I know the laws of renunciation. Yet winter encourages love to sweet hedonism. The cold in the distant corners of the room makes us love the fire that blazes at the center. Come, December! We want to snuggle, once again, beneath an afghan and hypnotize our souls with dancing flames. Here love feeds best. Warm bread is so tasteless in summer. Stars never really shine until the snow has cleaned the air; then distant galaxies bleed through the cold skies, and silence absorbs all sounds and starlight.

A thousand trials were ours from winter unto winter.

Did not our mothers die in those fast-fleeing seasons? Did not our unborn children come and grow in the wiry shadows of ourselves? Wasn't there a war in Southeast Asia? Six presidents came and went throughout those years. Yet two diamonds bound the decades neatly for the keeping of our hearts.

A COVENANT FOR ALL SEASONS

looks, the heavy footfalls, the silences, the small contests, the flashes of resentment; these all became a part
of our lives. We didn't know this was a regular part of
raising children. Still, for me, the years were a time of
unending strain. And for us, I could tell that the struggles of adolescence drove wedges of pain between us.
Motherhood is a category that sides deeply and consis-
tently with adolescence. Fatherhood gets tired quicker.
Motherhood understands when fatherhood rages.
Motherhood is willing to give situations another
chance, forgiving seventy times seven. Fatherhood de-
clares itself, legislates, and makes rules that often seal
the children away from themselves.

To be sure, children must be their own persons, and
I have always desired mine to be. But I found that
their seize-and-destroy path to the twenties passed
haltingly the broad fields of anger and moved out into
the deserts of silence.

You always seemed to handle so much more than I
could. You always believed that someday it would be
as it once was. You trusted that when they had laid
aside their need to contest every decision, to cut their
way to independence, life would be sweet again. You
trusted the message of Mark Twain's dictum that, once
they were a little older, they would see how very intel-
ligent we had become—all at once.

116

I can see that in most ways their challenges were normal. They never trespassed civil law nor declared themselves communists or ran off with lovers to live soap-opera lives. They never forced us to reckon with damaged reputations. They generally studied hard, made good grades, and enjoyed college.

But the deepest contests were always rooted in issues of their destinies. What could they have become if they had dreamed better? What were they contemplating that might hurt their studies or their futures? Their hostility rose quickly and seemed without a foundation. They may have confronted us so often just because we were there. It was their way of grasping greedily at the reins of family life. They had a way of making the least matters seem like power struggles, yet it always seemed to me that we were gentle in our use of power.

It was not our confrontations with them that began at last to weary me. It was the fact that I felt fatigue edging into our own relationship. The bright conversations of early marriage seemed to degenerate into business as usual. Dutifully we went to band concerts or choral concerts at school. The football games and dances that you often chaperoned were for me not so much wearisome as an intrusion into a busy church schedule that left us so little time for ourselves.

Our lawn was big and I gave myself to the dreary mowing of it. Our agenda grew mundane: the house, the laundry, the work you did constantly at school in the mornings and in the evenings; the church, the counseling appointments, the business meetings, the conventions; the days that kept us so busy they ended with our collapsing into bed at night.

I remembered so often during those days the myth of Sisyphus. I can see the titan: damned as he was to an eternity of misery, his crime so offensive to the gods that he was sentenced to a meaninglessness from which there was no exit. He must roll a huge boulder up the slopes of a steep mountain, only to watch it tumble and roll to the bottom again. Then he must descend the mountain and push it up again and so on, forever.

Meaninglessness always has no exit—no reasonable way out. I could picture this hulk of a demigod, straining his whole body, lifting and pushing and daring to believe there was meaning in the moment. His cheek against the stone, his foot wedging it in, all to bear it to the top one more weary time. How many times in eternity does he reach the meaningless summit? In the unholy humdrum, there is no difference between the top and the bottom. There are no goals, no prizes in such a predictable world.

But those years taught me much about the nature of life. Its great curse is never the effort, but the unanswered effort. No wonder Sartre defined the "hero" as the man who could look at the meaningless-ness of life and decide to keep on living.

To climb from a pit, one must ever remember the steep sides and convince himself that the tiny fleck of light high above must not be lost. For when the climb is over, that barely visible pinpoint of light will open into a world of sky and earth where the grass is tender and the world is young and hope is as certain as the breeze.

Sensitivity may be my own similarity to Sisyphus— my boulder on the slopes of the hill. I feel things so deeply. My depression settles ever deeper than yours. My elation rises higher—or so it seems on the surface. I articulate quickly what you ponder and often leave unsaid. Because of my own visible moods, my utter rejection of the routine is outwardly more venomous. I began to see why so many men in the twentieth year of marriage could no longer cope with the fatigue of their homes, where they felt they made mortgage pay-ments, but held no place.

Now that I really consider it, I realize you bore your own separate loneliness. You reached regularly to sta-bilize the children as they teetered on the various precipices of their teenage years. Yet at the same time, you tried to teach me to celebrate the ordinary things, so they might bring me more joy.

It began to occur to me: Sisyphus was more than a myth. Like me, he took himself too seriously. Could it be that he enjoyed his life of exhibitionism and even gloried in his observable pain? Was not some of the tedium of life his own fault? Could he not see it? There *must* have come a butterfly to rest upon his stone at some time. And maybe for one moment, the humdrum was enlivened by bright transcendent wings.

During one of the seasons of drudgery I wrote my reflections on Sisyphus.

We are tied to micro-tasks: bitter vinegar and gall,
Hoping for the larger moments, doomed to
     live among the small.

We would be presidents or kings, building towers
     for artful skies,
Smiling while the pawns hack pawns, for the
     bishops' enterprise.

But the laundry! God, the laundry! Done a
     thousand times, but here once more.
The factory eating up our stamina with rivets,
     driven hard with heat and gore.
In the same plates, mind you, that we've
     riveted before.
Rivets, hundreds of them, years and years of rivets . . . .

Sisyphus, you blind and mundane dolt! You missed the butterfly. So had I. The tedium was not our curse, nor was the children's adolescence. The curse, like the blessing, lay within ourselves, because we so willingly enter the dull and dangerous dungeons of our hearts.

The tedium that we so despise is not our curse but our salvation. The lawn and the laundry redeem us. At last, I could see that the product is the tedium. The regularity of things that must be done often mortars our souls into union. We could be healed. Jesus said:

Consider the lilies of the fields, how they grow;
they toil not, neither do they spin: And yet I say
unto you, That even Solomon in all his glory
was not arrayed like one of these (Matt. 6:28-29).

I saw you again in a new way the summer that our children finished high school. We were in the mountains. Do you remember the field of sego lilies? I looked at the small exquisite flowers, and in them, I understood the glory of our freedom. Here lay the truth of the summer of 1980: There are no anxious lilies. They bear no strain—debate no longing views of life. There are only free, white flowers that work together to blanket a mountainside. "Yet Solomon in all his glory was not arrayed like one of these."

I knew the stress within our marriage could be put to rest if I would pull down the high walls of my demands. In the pain of their growing, our children were becoming what we were: adults. I smiled. I knew that this was exactly how they saw us. They were becoming adults, and we were only becoming old. What a foolish misjudgment was theirs!

Now I could tell them. There are no adults. Adults are only older children who reach out for love and cry out to be touched. Adults are not postadolescents, not beings cured of teenager-hood. Adults are caught in the lifelong struggle of wondering what to do with their maturity. They are always plagued by feelings that they too are children forced to dress up and play for real at a game they barely understand. They ache in the realization that the bright prophecies of their youth are not being fulfilled. Our new resolve was declared neither to ourselves nor to our children. The days sped by. The laundry came and went by loads. The lawn mowers did their work. Yet there was a freshness along our well-trodden paths. We were free as the lilies. We had given life our best effort, and the best product was our children. Our son joined the army and our daughter continued on in school. Both at once? Why? They were trying to leave childhood only to find that they could never leave. But like Hansel and

Gretel, they became confident in their trust that even in the midst of a dark forest, the witches could all be beaten.

Not my blood

The doctors like stern prophets prophesied
That barrenness would curse our anxious hope
And heritage. But see the prophets lied—
A dark skinned child came like an infant pope,
To bless the multitudes with open joy.
I never stop to wonder at God's grace
Until I see this primal, brown-eyed boy,
In him God's love acquired a face.
Not of my blood you say? Idolatry
Of genes and DNA. This child I so esteem
Has magic power, and has demandingly
Reduced the great Pacific to a stream.
He tricked the ocean into shallow shoals
Then waded it across to claim our souls.

CHAPTER FIFTEEN

Grandparents

There is a sharp sting in the words "I'm sorry, but you will never have children." It is not a statement that terminates life, but it amputates our best hopes. When our daughter's physician gave the unkind words to her, she felt that blade-in-the-gut denial of her future. But even more than that, she felt as though her sense of promise to us was also violated. It was not that some out-loud commitment she had made to us was broken. She felt she had violated a glorious expectation.

Grandparenting is the grand finale of all parenting. It is rarely a grand promise that children make to their parents. But it is a grand assumption; sterility and barrenness form the dry moat around such castles of expectation.

Doctors always begin these doleful cycles of pronouncement by telling the never-to-be parents. They inform the never-to-be grandparents. Bit by bit the dour news filters like ice water through family reunions and that "now-now-deary-it's-not-all-that-bad" circle of friends.

The shame that barren couples feel is a whispered whipping of egos. It resides as an inner remorse for some foolish sin they have been charged with but never committed. "You're not normal," it says to wives who can't be mothers. "If only you were more of a man," it scorns husbands who can't be fathers. "Too bad for you," it snivels at aging couples. "Get a dog, a goldfish, and die."

So our children told us the news—the bad news. There were tears, of course, but then they said, "Is it okay, Mom and Dad?" What they really meant was, "Are *we* still okay?"

"It's just fine and you're just fine, and we're just fine," we said. "Nothing has changed."

But they knew and we knew. It was like we all agreed to close a little window in our favorite part of the house. We had looked out that window so often. Through its beckoning we saw vistas of simplicity and warmth. We all could see a baby playing in the sun. We beheld the child growing. We needed this little one to promise us continuance on the earth. *Progeny* is the three-syllable way to spell *hope*. It comes with the promise that through your children your life goes on beyond you. It is the blood serum and DNA promise. When that child played outside tomorrow's window, we knew why Old Testament patriarchs kept their genealogies and talked about the seventh son of the seventh son. It is not eternal life to see our children's children having children. But there is a simple wonder in knowing that through God and genetics we are extending our mortal lives beyond ourselves.

The child in our future was suddenly gone. Now outside that once hopeful window were only distant graves, first ours, then our children's. There the lineage stopped. None beyond our own children would continue the life our grandparents had passed on to our parents, and which we had passed on to our children.

There was no child in the garden.

There was no garden.

Finally, there was no window.

It was as though the antigenealogy demon had come and taken out the window and sealed the wall . . . the dark wall! But the pronouncement welded our intention that life would not dictate our joy. We turned away from our despairing mood, promising ourselves we would never again look at the dark wall.

We turned our hearts from thinking of the joy we could never own. We all had things to do. Our jobs were there daily and we did them. Church was there weekly and we worshiped. The seasons changed every three months, and we blessed the changes. Christmases came and we celebrated them. Life was full of variety. We laughed our way along as we sampled all of it.

Then a wonderful idea was born. You, our children, heard of a little baby born oceans away from us, half-way around the world. "A child was born," you told us. A simple litany of four words. But it sounded like you had stolen it from the Christmas chapter of St. Luke's Gospel. "A child is born," you might have said, like noels sung in August. "A child . . . not in Bethle-hem but in India—near Calcutta." So stars do shine and shepherds are amazed in dark fields, and Christ-mases can come to the ordinary and the needy.

Your simple words flew at us with new hope. "In that section of India where there was no grain, where famine kills," you said, "a mother died of malnutrition. The child born at her death weighed only three pounds, and was in a rural Indian hospital. He was from a Hindu caste where he would never be permitted to go to school, even if he were lucky enough to live. We'd like to try to adopt him. What do you think? How would you feel about having an adopted grandson?"

"Do not even ask," we said, "Just open our world with such a dream as this."

We knew in our hearts that this was not just a way to get a grandson, it was somehow glorious and Christlike. It was an issue bigger than family or prejudice or social expectations. Would we like an adopted child? It was as though two great things were born in us at once. It was a chance to have a child to love, but even more than that it was a way to confer upon this child a reason to be all he might be. This caste-locked child could be educated. He would not have to fear dying from hunger as his biological mother had done. "Yes, do it . . . now," we encouraged you.

The window was back. Now there was a brown-skinned child playing in the garden. It was Christ Himself who came to cut the new window in the dark wall. And when the window was there once again He pointed outside and said to us, "Look! There he is. Be rich once more with dreams. The hope you thought was gone is yet alive."

Then between their dreams began the thousand ups-and-downs of waiting to be sure our dreams had substance. Paperwork—family studies—paperwork—initial payments to the agency—paperwork—three weeks of nothing. It wasn't going to work, was it? We were a family of fools bent upon an unrealistic hope of ever moving the Indian government to care. India was a strong nation of almost one billion people, and millions of children. Now she was refusing to give us even one.

More studies—more waiting—more silence—no letters in the post—paperwork. And now the child we waited to adopt was four months old or dead or quite alive or never leaving Calcutta. *It's best not to hope,* we told ourselves; *it makes the dreaming cheaper.* No dreams are ever quite so costly as those we pump with our anticipation. *We must give up . . . que será, será.* Fine, there's an end of hoping—a long five months.

Then presto! More pictures of Sangram! How beautiful the child. Hurry into the village—wake the town and tell the people! It will happen! Hope was not a dry well. It is a fountain rich with cold, deep joy. The window once again is in the dark wall—our child is playing again in tomorrow's garden.

So went our lives on a never-ending roller coaster of exhilaration and discouragement. We sent the baby clothes and very simple gifts at the encouragement of the Indian orphanage where he lived. We never knew when he got them or *if* he got them. More months. Now he was one year old! More money was required, more studies. More of our frazzled emotional souls was used as currency for the transaction.

Waiting needs reinforcement at times. We bought a baby bed and painted up the nursery, with stenciled infantile acrylic bears. This room became the focus while we waited. This bright red baby bed would be the control panel which pushed the buttons of our existence. Then came the greatest, final act of faith. They asked us to send the money for two halfway-around-the-world airfares—one for the baby, now thirteen months old, and one for a Mr. Mohapatra, who would be bringing him to America.

Then came the best of letters! He was coming. We had a flight number and a plane to meet. The baby, at fourteen months, was to make an eight-hour jeep ride through the back section of India, where the orphanage was located, to the airport in Calcutta. There he would fly on various flights to Washington, D.C. and finally he would land at Omaha's Eppley Airfield. He was coming by way of the sky—and we were ecstatic.

The day came!

We all went as families and as friends to bow, like swarming magi, before this infant—this high-tech, jet-propelled infant—this child of rural India—this son of turbine engines—this final wondrous end of all our hopes. We gathered by fifties at the airport, amassing like Turks along the runways. We peered out the windows through streaming rain. The runways were wet, not icy. The plane was two hours late.

We were worn out with waiting, but we ran from the runway side of the airport to the jet-way side of the airport. Oh no! It was Jet-way 13! We were not superstitious, but 13! What if he wasn't on the plane? We couldn't think about it.

People began to disembark from the packed plane. So many unnecessary passengers! Who were all these people, casually walking off the jet-way? What right did they have to preempt our joy? Why were there so many eccentrics talking too loudly? There were nicotine habituates waiting to smoke! A nun, mind you! A woman of God, purposefully in our way. Two red-faced, John Wayne-looking men, talking to a mustached third, who looked like the godfather. Three noisy kids who seemed dear to their mothers but hardly to anyone else.

We sorted through all these, looking for a turbaned man from India with a child. Then there came out a handsome Indian. We broke into applause. He was wearing a turban but had no baby. He looked oddly at his fifty-person reception committee and smiled as if to say, "Hey, what a welcome. I love this country!"

Then we smiled, realizing it was not him.

Finally everyone was off the plane. What? No one else? Soon the pilots and stewardesses would be walking off. Wait—a short man came last and quite separate from the rest. It was him—a short, dark-skinned man carrying a wonderful dark-eyed child.

Now came the world's greatest sufferance. Two sets of grandparents, straining with eyes round like lemurs on a midnight moon. How we wanted to touch the child and be healed of our madness! But we had all rehearsed our forbearance. None but his MOTHER would hold him for the first week!

We must allow them to meet—the child and his MOTHER. No one else must add to the child's confusion. Grandparents beware! Fold your hooks, you vampires. Do not reach. Try not to touch. Enjoy the glory, but wait your turn. Let MOTHER AND CHILD declare their love. Then in a week, or a month, your turn will come. Despising our commitments, we waited.

And THUS THE MIRACLE!

The man advanced. EAST met WEST. He handed our daughter a tiny boy—a child whose almond eyes were lit with Indian fire an ocean away . . . on the other side of the planet.

The baby—God be praised—did not recoil: his little arms reached out to a woman nourished all her life on fast foods and Western civilization. He held her neck as if to say, "I've waited all my life to find you." She kissed him and he smiled a baby's smile as if to say, "How nice, Mother." Then he looked out at the sea of big-eyed self-despisers who had watched his "splash down" in the Western world as if to say, "Mother, these people bother me; could we go home now?"

Not quite yet.

First must come the odd ritual of our beginning. The new mother knew his diaper was unchanged. Here was the test. She laid him down, in the circle of observers, and took off his diaper. It was dingy—perhaps because it had been washed only on some river bank never knowing borax. Now comes a snow white diaper, and then—welcome to the West, young man!—tiny Star Wars pajamas, complete with R-2-D-2s and Yodas!

And so the Jedi knight had landed. The era of the child was born into our lives. It continues to this day. And Christmas is better than it's ever been. Disney World was born again for us. Sangram was named Jared, which goes much better with Star Wars pajamas. And in time, Jared became a baby citizen, falling asleep under the American flag and a huge picture of the Statue of Liberty.

But better than all these little joys is the window in the dark wall which is now always full of light. Now it is Jared's sixth year, and we have learned to sing with the psalmist:

Children are an heritage of the Lord . . .
Happy is the man that hath his quiver full of them.
(Ps. 127:3-4)

THE BURNOUT TO GLORY

"Upon this rock I'll build!" You said. "Who me?
My stone," I cried, "is too unsure to stand.
Please. Find another rock and let me be."
There's no foundation underneath the sand
Of my frail faith. They lie who say they know
My light can make converts efficiently—
And I can stand against the dark! Not so!
Moral needy night depresses me.
Yet I layed by this threat'ning fearsome part.
He came and spoke, and in His countermand
He, the Enabler, reached and took my heart
And you, dear saint, reached out and took my hand.
The decades rolled! Your strength remained in place.
You brought me joy and He supplied the grace.

CHAPTER SIXTEEN

The Needy Evermore

The year 1990 saw us in our early fifties and nearing the end of our long love affair with our congregation. What we could not know was that this grueling divorce with our twenty-five-year old mate would be more ripping for us than for them. I never realized till then just how much Jesus loved His church—indeed, she was His bride. But I had rarely stopped to consider how much *I* loved His church.

I had served His church, running to meet her every need while she grew from ten members to three thousand. After my twenty-five year marriage to His bride, I found myself growing very bitter. I still believed she was His bride, but I often found her not so much to my liking. She was once a small and warm fellowship that met my needs while I met hers. Now Christ's bride, once a joyous and petite companion, had become an oversized, demanding woman. Whatever I did to try to please her was never enough. When I was tired, she collected the last drop of my stamina, then reprimanded me because I had nothing more to give.

I cannot doubt now that much of this was my fault. When the church was little, I had time to care for everyone and I ran quickly to sit and pray at the side of every human need. As it grew larger I ran faster, sitting a little less each time. As I ran faster my prayers grew shorter, my visits more hurried, and my days much longer. When I first became pastor, I loved to hear their affirmation, "How good of you to come, pastor—you never forget." I was addicted to congregational compliments.

I would pass two of them in the hall and overhear them saying, "The pastor never fails to attend our needs—he's a wonderful man." I know flattery for what it is, and I would always think to myself, *I'm not all that wonderful but I am faithful to my flock.* But as the passing of the years changed into decades, my fatigue level often demanded that I quit earlier in the evening. Guilt followed me home on these evenings. In such a large church, I never went to bed without thinking of all the needy I hadn't seen. More and more their compliments turned to criticism.

It was then I sinned against Christ. I had once said that those genuine ministers who really served the Lord could never experience pastoral burnout. Indeed, when any pastor told me he had "had it" with church and was throwing in the towel, I would say, "There goes one shallow person. Were he as deeply devoted as I am, he would serve and never quit." My congregation's frequent compliments, coupled with my belief that quitters were shallow men, brought me at last to my deplorable state of confusion.

Barbara, how much your love meant to me during those awful seasons of stress. You had now been my mate of thirty-five years, most all of which we had lived out together in this one church. I loved you more and more even as I began to turn from the church. You never added to my burden, nor tried to advise me spiritually. You were just there, ready to lift me up in prayer and support me in my wearisome calling.

We both noticed, however, that the church was so all-consuming in her demands that she unwittingly drove a wedge deep into the heart of our union. She couldn't threaten us into a divorce court, but she did effect a kind of spiritual and philosophical divorce. She separated us into two separate people, one of which stayed home alone and the other which ran furiously to tend to her all-demanding agenda. The church as the bride of Christ I increasingly saw as a sick woman . . . a growing invalid. She got bigger and bigger, she just never got well. She finally became a thick, critical matron who rarely said anything nice.

I do not say she ever looked sick; she always looked well. As American suburbanite Christians measured health, she was quite vital. She had craft shows, casserole dinners without number, and softball teams uncountable. Those who were prone to champion her size pointed out how well the fund-raising program had gone or how much they enjoyed the latest style show. Meanwhile, underneath the hurried surface I worked. There were several other ministers at the church who could go and tend to needs, but I was the one who *had* to go.

I learned how we ministers may trade our service unto Christ alone for such a small thing as congregational goodwill. I once had ministered to become His hands and feet in the needy world. Then as the church grew—somewhere as it grew—I began to minister to the god of goodwill. Finally, I was running merely to try and shut the flood gates of pastoral criticism.

I quit writing! There was no time for it. The voracious demands of His huge and critical bride left me no time to write. After she was through with me for the day, I was too tired to write. I read very little. I got up in the morning, put on a suit and tie—my clerical uniform of the day—and asked, "Which way am I to run today, Lord?" Only now and then did I ask Malcom Boyd's fearful question, "Are you running with me, Jesus?" I know now that most of the time He was not running with me; I ran alone.

I thought of David Brainerd's reputed lament. This great hero among colonial believers died quite young. His lament was that he had killed himself with holy intentions. He made his body a horse in metaphor. "God gave me a horse to ride and a message to preach," he said. "Alas, I have killed the horse and cannot deliver the message." I realized I was headed for an early death if I did not quit serving the god of whirl and give my life again to Jesus.

I thought of the passage, "Thou wilt keep him in perfect peace, whose mind is stayed on thee" (Isa. 26:3). I had no peace. I actually hated my job. I walked a slack and dangerous tightrope between the Christ I never ceased to love and the church I more and more disliked.

I once had a good friend who resigned from his very large church. When I asked him why, he told me a tale that sounded very much like my own. He was being busied into agnosticism. For the sake of his own walk with Christ he had to rediscover the youthful, sensitive soul he also had lost in shallow turbulence of his own grumbling Galilee. Like me, he still admired the Christ who walked on water, but found himself unable even to wade through the brackish, ensnaring waters of his own parish. Finally, he told me that while he didn't hate anybody in particular, he just couldn't tolerate their massive togetherness. Individually he loved them, but united he at first had feared them and at last deplored them. He reached the place where his grudges wouldn't sleep. Finally, he said that even as he came over the hill and saw his church building he would begin getting physically ill. And so he at last denied his church, resigned his pulpit, and began reaching out to try to find God once again.

In many ways his testimony became increasingly my own. When we first built our huge, final sanctuary on a prominent hilltop, I felt the pride that Cheops must have felt when he watched the fellahin build the greatest pyramid of all. Like most pastors of large and growing churches, I had never wanted to be a monument builder. But pride intervened. The marvelous steeple was visible all over town. And after all, as I had so adeptly argued with the building committee, "A steeple is a finger that always points to God." The building committee had pointed out that ours was quite "a large and expensive finger." But I said, "So it will point out a large and powerful God." Still in my heart I slowly changed my mind about the new steeple. At first, I was proud that I could see it as I ran all over town. But gradually it seemed to quit pointing up to God and began wagging at me. Wherever I was in the community it seemed to scold me across the rooftops, "Why aren't you going faster, man; you know how much there is to do." Because the parsonage was right behind the church, the finger of God would appear through my bathroom window and fall in the glass right beside my face as I shaved each morning. My FACE and the STEEPLE always together. As I started any day it shook its long, rebuking finger in my face and said, "Hurry up, man; what do you think you are, a layman?" As I hurried faster I would always think, *Ah, shut up and go back to pointing at God.* We are in a most lamentable state when we start talking back to steeples, but that's how I was—a man living on the ragged edge.

In this schizophrenic state I realized that the church and I were like so many marriages I had seen: we were still living together, but we were not speaking. A part of the problem was that I loved the church and had given up twenty-five years of my life in adoration. Further, I had sacrificed my family's time and given it so much of our money that I had never prepared adequately for my retirement years. The church had been most remiss in not providing an annuity program for me. Its failure to provide for our retirement may have fueled the grudge that inhabited my fifty-fifth year.

All in all, it was easy to see—at least in my mind's eye—that the romance we once enjoyed was dead.

This would be proved a few months later when our twenty-fifth anniversary at the church came and went without mention. I saw this as a clear signal that our love affair was over. When any marriage crosses its silver anniversary with no acknowledgment of the day, the marriage is irretrievably dead. I did not spend my grudge with delight. I was usually too tired to cry over it. Fatigue forbids emotion. TIRED kills everything, and I was tired.

This madness might have gone on forever except for December of 1990. Coupled with a choir pageant, with rehearsals claiming the early part of the month and performances the last, came a most tiresome crisis. One of the Bible study classes was angry with the youth director and decided to end their relationship with the church. I had mixed emotions about the secessionist group. I knew the youth director was innocent of their criticisms, but it was ever so refreshing to have them mad at someone besides myself.

This scenario I had dealt with several times across the years. I feared that no amount of pleading could call them back. Still I tried. I injected the lost, but noble, effort into the maelstrom of December church programming. In a month where every night is scheduled with parties, receptions, programs, and services, I spent my days trying to save a group that was leaving the church with display and great noise. They were not to be saved.

Decembers always faded into Januarys. But in the year's mad and spastic dying, we arrived disconsolately at January 1991. It was not a bright new year. It was only another one. The church would get bigger; we would run faster. Considering the December which had gone before, you, dear wife, spoke to me some very haunting words, "You know, we never had a Christmas of our own this year." I realized that you spoke the truth. Between trying to save a very angry Bible class and being sure that everyone else at the church had a Christmas with everything in place, we had had no Christmas of our own.

A new and firm decision began forming inside of me: I would leave the church. I would dissolve this tasteless, twenty-five-year-old marriage. The bride of Christ, I acknowledged, was only my mistress. The bride of Christ a mistress! How obscene that I had permitted her loud demands to nibble at our own union. She could not destroy the legality of our marriage, but she had eaten at its heart until she had devoured all the vitality out of our relationship.

This was a decision I made clearly and firmly. I had known many "Monday morning resignations." Every pastor feels these as he reckons with the church's demands and his own fatigue. But this was more than that. It wasn't just that we had not had Christmas in December, but that we had no home life or marriage the rest of the year. Christ never demanded that we trade our marriage for a ministry gone mad. He had called us into union and blessed our marriage with his holy light. No, it was not just for our sake we had to leave the church. It was for His sake. I thought of Nietzsche's cry, "I deny God for His sake." My own cry grew out of my need to separate Christian busyness from Christ. I knew I must find Christ. I cried with Job, "Oh that I knew where I might find him!" (Job 23:3).

In my desperation I returned again and again to Kavanaugh's *The Birth of God*. When Kavanaugh finally gained the courage to leave the priesthood, he confessed that God was born in him. I, likewise, knew that somewhere beyond suburban "busianity" I would find both you and Him once again. Now the hunger in me grew.

Oh how I wanted to find you again. It was not because I had served Christ with such intensity that I had lost you. It was that I had served the church so insanely that I had lost you both. I made up my mind in January to leave the pulpit I had assumed some twenty-five years earlier. As if God understood, the unfolding weeks thereafter revealed a host of new opportunities. I had several job offers to teach or work in a university or graduate school. By November of that year, I had secured a teaching position and had resigned.

I had always told myself that resigning the pulpit would be hard to do, but it was not the chore I had imagined. It released in us an incredible lightness of being and freedom. It was odd that the resignation brought an instant flood of dinner invitations and receptions. We were hosted at a final reception with a couple of thousand friends stopping by to tell us how much we had meant to them. I wonder why they hadn't told us that for years. Finally they gave us a special offering of several thousand dollars. The bitterness I felt was wrapped in warm farewells. As Juliet said, "Parting is such sweet sorrow."

Nonetheless, for us the parting sweetness was more pronounced than all the final sorrow. We left Nebraska for a position at a seminary in Texas. And how shall I say it—we were free. We were young and in love again. Euphoria was as bright as the headlights that guided us down the road away from Nebraska, our home of more than thirty years.

I was guided by two bits of verse I knew. There really was a land of beginning again, as Louise Fletcher described:

I wish that there were some wonderful place
  Called the Land of Beginning Again,
Where all of our mistakes and all our heartaches
  And all of our poor selfish grief
Could be dropped like a shabby old coat at the door,
  And never be put on again.

And the second was the marvelous words of Charles Wesley, in what I suddenly saw as my hymn of liberation. I sang it inwardly over and over, all the way to our new home in Texas.

Long my imprisoned spirit lay
Fast bound in sin and nature's night;
Thine eye diffused a quick'ning ray,
I woke, my dungeon flamed with light;
My chains fell off, my heart was free.
I rose, went forth, and followed thee.

TOMBSTONE SHOPPING

Today we bought a space beyond the tree—
Beyond the stones we set but yesterday
For those who claimed their immortality
Ahead. The church is but a mile away
Where we made promises in candlelight.
Time urged and we sped past that May
By forty years. Like actors with stage fright
Before the timid ending of a play.
We know that one of us must finish first,
And one bring roses to the curtain call.
Love's sudden crepe finale unrehearsed
Demands we live until that curtain falls.
Let's hold each other till the edge of night;
Our encores will be born in better light.

CHAPTER SEVENTEEN

Final Thanks

After all these years, I wonder now at my reluctance to become engaged to you. The love I struggled to define, defined itself in time. We celebrate our growth by smiling at our outgrown concepts. We have lived together long enough to know that we were made to live together. Gone is any false attempt to recreate each other in some image that we might find more acceptable. Once we left our need to change each other, we were free to celebrate ourselves as we are.

We are gloriously together and it is not dull company. We are filled with a fullness that guards against its own spillage. When we are together, we are content because our communication needs no larger audience than ourselves. We have learned that loneliness inhabits crowds.

Remember the cataracts of Niagara? The falls flowed on, like time itself. Our marriage, like that river, ever seeks a wider place. The dark cascades that roared across our early years have now moved on. There is a crispness already in the air that reminds us that we cannot have summer forever. Our former woes may at last give way to bigger ones—maybe disease, perhaps infirmity. One day, one of us will be forced to stand alone and test the shattering emptiness that is the final fruit of those who have known intimate closeness.

Are we up to the future? We must not be frightened by those fears that make us die before we've lived each day to the fullest. We must be fully alive in the present and stay alive until we have to say good-bye. Someone once remarked that the future is much like the present—only longer. Neither the future nor the present is a terror to those who walk as one.

Our commitments were never showy. I rarely chose to give you kisses or gifts in public. We kept the best events of life between ourselves. We are still at our best when we are alone, neither observed nor exhibitionist in our loving. We rarely spend our substance in giving lavish gifts. Time together is the grand gift—yes, and being. There is no need for presents when life itself is a present.

Even now as I write, I know the children will soon be home for the holidays. And shortly after Christmas, the holiday will end upon a midnight. On that eve, the clock will remind us that another year has dawned. It will bid us to stay alive by honoring some old and certain covenants. The midnight clock will remind us that time is a gift to keep only while we live, and live we shall. As the ghost of Christmas Present reminded Ebenezer: "There is never enough time and suddenly you're not there anymore." But the shortness of life will not hurry us into moroseness. We will seek joy without cramming all the goodies of this life too quickly into our pockets, as though there was no more. To understand the swiftness of life is to live in youth. And sometimes I think we are younger in our fifties than we ever were in early marriage.

And in the cycle of change, each year—with its beauty and intrigue—will pass on, stealing the years from us as we celebrate its passage. Since first we met, a hundred seasons have come and gone, each one summoning up our great desire to meet the next.

Our greatest joys are simple: the stone hearth in February, the small fountain on our patio, the flowering crab apple tree, the walks in summer, the fall colors of the river forests we love. These joys celebrate the past as we reach ahead with eagerness. Living fully in the now is the only way to keep the years from becoming the skeletons of old, dull schedules.

Let me watch you making tea on cold mornings. Tease the puppy in the garden. Cover the geraniums against first frost. I want to watch these simple acts mortar moments into life. Thus is tomorrow born again, ninety times in every season.

Long ago I wrote these words to you—on the occasion of our twenty-fifth anniversary:

OF TIME AND DIGNITY

With dignity you dress the grace you own
More fully with each passing year. And I
Stand near, as season passes season by—
Uncounted, unexamined, left alone.
To be forgotten? No! See how life goes?
The time must not be worshiped. Decades must
Be warmly worn and somehow left in trust
As strength for other trials and later foes.
Still I'll not wish for us some candled night
Of ceremonies gone. Life's now! Life's here!
We still are one to stand astride the years.
We've seen the dark, yet celebrate the light.
The years between what was and is to be
Are but the preface to eternity.

In Robert Browning's words I have found the finishing epigraph of our desires: "Grow old with me, the best is yet to be." Recently we walked in a small cemetery not a mile from where we were married. It was much like Emily's delirious death-dream, in the play *Our Town*. We saw there the graves of our family and many friends. Here your grandfather lies. He was carried into Oklahoma Territory during the Land Run of 1893, a century ago. He only died a couple of years ago and his life, at 102 years of age, defines the whole history of Oklahoma. His prairie-ginghamed Edith—his bride of frontier dreams—lies there beside him. She too watched horse-and-buggy-buckboard days give way to automobiles. Here lie your father's parents, and someday your father will lie here as well. And a double score of other folks we knew. We now own some lots here beside your mother, and just a little earthen distance from your grandfather. All in all, it is a heady place to "wait the trumpet," among a sea of friends.

In this familiar sea of gravestones, we decided to buy cemetery lots for that time we would leave the earth for brighter, better realms. We promised that we would say something nice about each other on the stones that will show our children where to lay their flowers. Who knows how often our own children will come? They each live several hundred miles away. But no matter. This portion of the wide world is ours. This quiet place of thin-clad prairie junipers and three-strand, barbed-wire fences, of green wheat grown in chocolate earth, and red shale roads, this prairie potter's field is where we'll be. This is the place we grew up. Here we were once young; here we will be when we are young no longer. And like a magnet we feel the pull of this finality, drawing at us most powerfully.

There is that old Scottish legend that tells of two brothers who fought side by side until one of them was killed in battle, away from home. All Scots believed you were obligated to be buried at home in Scotland. Those who could get there while they were alive were said to have taken the "high road" home to die. Those who miscalculated when their end would come, and were caught dying a long way from home were said to have taken the "lower road." But no matter, the lower road was quicker even than the higher, and thus the lucky dead brother reached the home soil first. It really didn't matter, goes the song. The lure of the homeland was so powerful that all roads led at last to the "bonny, bonny banks of Loch Lomond." There is a homing instinct in the human spirit that bids us finish life where we began it.

There is a bizarre romance born in graveyards. We all idealize the dead and speak well of them. Their memory evokes in us a charity we never had while they were alive. No tombstone ever tells the whole truth about a rogue. Even those not-so-dear we once tried to like, are suddenly the "dearly departed." We both agree that romantic notions of the idea of dying are much too sweet. And yet these very strange romantic ideas bless the concept of being dead. But we are decided—high road or low—here in this simple, lonely, prairie place we will one day lie.

The experiences of life hurry us far faster than we would like toward that little "field of dreams." Now as our children hurry on toward middle age, and our grandson is in school, we honestly confess that we dread the possibilities that in the future these hurried days will pass us up and leave us very much alone in that far-distant, prairie place.

It's odd that we, not quite six decades wise, have never thought of ourselves as old. To me you're still that blushing and coy girl who took my ring and name, and then agreed to explore the world with me. We conquered and claimed what little territories we could. And now, my darling, we realize the lands where we planted our frail flags to mark our little kingdoms are soon to pass. But for a while we dreamed, we loved, we worshiped, and we were.

I see you still in May 1959, coming down the aisle in white, alive, quite young, most beautiful, and best of all, in love. These are the images I cannot surrender. Neither could Leigh Hunt. Thinking of his young bride in old age he wrote:

Jenny kiss'd me when we met,
Jumping from the chair she sat in;
Time, you thief, who love to get
Sweets into your list, put that in!
Say I'm weary, say I'm sad,
Say that health and wealth have miss'd me,
Say I'm growing old, but add,
Jenny kiss'd me.

I woke on a recent morning before you. The early sunlight streaming through the glass fell upon your hair and hands. I reached and touched your hand made noble by its years of service. An old song came to mind I hadn't thought of in years:

These hands aren't the hands of a gentleman
These hands are withered with care
These hands raised a family
These hands built a home
Now these hands are raised to God in prayer.

The poetry lacks excellence; the theology is poor, but I touched your hand that morning to realize that at least the sentiment of the tune was on target. I loved you, and the warm sun on your skin called to remembrance all that we have shared these past thirty-six years. Pardon me if I—as I always have done—oversentimentalize our love affair.

Mark Twain was born in the year of Halley's Comet, and pledged to all his friends he would see it come again. Its seventy-five-year orbit folded over both ends of his life and he made good his pledge. I make you no promises about how long I shall live. We have now only a few years before A.D. 2000. Who can say what the third millennium will offer us? I cannot say if we shall even be here, but if so we will have been married forty-one years and I will be near retirement age.

It is morose for us to reckon with the years. Did not the psalmist counsel us to number our days and so apply our hearts to wisdom? (Ps. 90:12). I am always haunted by that Goya painting we saw in the Prado. It was a dark canvas of the Roman god of time, entitled "Saturn Eating His Children." The painting is a likeness of a huge god devouring human beings, as indeed time does. The psalmist is not so defeatist, but he does remind us that we should spend our days aware that we cannot outrun the clock. Even our ever-circling Christmases point out the glaring truth that the clock always wins. We may only win if we arrive at our appointed time having accomplished all that God gave us to do.

The apostle Paul dramatically defeated the clock and he eloquently testified, "I have finished my course, I have kept the faith: Henceforth there is laid up for me a crown of righteousness, which the Lord, the righteous judge, shall give me at that day: and not to me only, but unto all them also who love his appearing" (2 Tim. 4:7-8). Time can never be the victor over those who have plotted against the hourglass with their faith. These step across the threshold of eternity with a gift they could not leave on earth, for their treasure was stored up in that clockless world of God's unending day.

Such treasure has been ours.

What treasure?

This gold is ours: Our children are both well and married. Our grandson can create Christmas from the most ordinary of days. We feel God's benediction in such simple things as teapots and novels. We are wealthy with a treasure *Forbes Magazine* has never named. And each day wakes us with the undiminished glory of our togetherness.

The number of our days will not come out the same. What's yours is mine and mine yours, on earth as it is in heaven. How I have loved thee, how I do love thee, and how I shall love thee are but three tenses of the timeless wealth we've held. I bring it now to remembrance, so that whichever one of us first reaches that prairie place, the other may celebrate our treasure with a transcending joy. We'll sorrow not as those who have no hope. Here then, I close this brief account of all our years by listing those treasures still held in our account.

I call to mind how first we met, for there
In that small Oklahoma town I held
You first in promises. The very air
Was sanctified by all that God compelled
Us to affirm. And even then you knew
You loved. So sure you were and so eighteen.
You held to all you felt. I married you.
Then I, at last, saw all that you had seen,
  This Gold is ours.
We knew the warm sweet sun of love in youth.
We felt the touch that gilded every night
With warmth. We drove each false thing out
  with truth
Till dark integrity recoiled before the light.
We loved each other with such honesty
That we lived poor but thought of it as wealth.
Our "yea was yea" and thus integrity
Blessed every day with trust and love with health.
  This Gold is ours.

The children came, but only to enhance
Our love. They came from God and so belonged
To him. We promised Him that our romance
Was born before they were. We would not wrong
Each other then by giving them that place
Of adoration in our heart of hearts
That we had pledged in holy grace.
To cherish is the altar of our art.

       This Gold is ours.

My darling, you have made me rich as Troy,
You crowned my being with such wealth
  piled high
I pitied men who never knew such joy.
And yet I must apologize that I
Was never able to rebuke the years
For their wild hurried pace and now we're old,
Old? No! For all the laughter and the tears
Are smelted into Heaven's finest gold.

       This Gold is ours.

Please, am I walking somewhat slower now?
It's not because I'm tired. It only seems
I'm dancing as my stamina allows.
No one walks fast who is weighted down
  with dreams.
Come walk with me, my love, but not too fast.
We will not pace ourselves because we're old.

There still are vistas we won't hurry past
And we will pace ourselves to bear the Gold
We know is ever ours.